A CROFT IN THE HILLS

Other books by Katharine Stewart include:

Crofts and Crofting
A Garden in the Hills
A School in the Hills
The Post in the Hills
The Crofting Way

A CROFT IN THE HILLS

KATHARINE STEWART

Foreword to the First Edition by
NEIL M. GUNN

Foreword to the Second Edition by
EONA MACNICOL

Illustrated by
ANNE SHORTREED

mercatpress
www.mercatpress.com

First published in 1960 by Oliver and Boyd
and reprinted in the same year
A new edition published by Melven Press in 1979
Reprinted by Mercat Press in 1991, 1994, 1998 and 2000
This edition reset and published in 2005 by Mercat Press
at 10 Coates Crescent, Edinburgh EH3 7AL
www.mercatpress.com

ISBN: 184183 0852

Set in Bembo 11pt at Mercat Press

Printed in Great Britain by
Bell & Bain Ltd., Glasgow

CONTENTS

TO MY FAMILY

'*All of you with little children . . . take them somehow into the country among green grass and yellow wheat— among trees—by hills and streams, if you wish their highest education, that of the heart and the soul, to be completed.*'
Richard Jefferies

INTRODUCTION
to the First Edition

WHY, you may ask, record the simple fact that three people took to the hills and lived quiet lives under a wide sky, among the rock and heather, working with the crops and beasts they could manage to raise there, in order to feed and clothe themselves. There is certainly little room for dramatic highlights in this story of ours. But we heard the singing and we found the gold. And I believe that each small stand taken against the shrill wind of disenchantment which is blowing across the world has more positive human value than many of the assertions being made by science today.

Science says: 'Here is a stone. It weighs so much. It measures so much. It is so-and-so many years old.' But a man needs to discover that the stone is strong, so that he can stand on it, and cool, so that he can lay his head against it: that it is beautiful and can be fashioned as an ornament, or hard and can be built into his home.

How does he make these discoveries? With his own eyes, his own wits, his own imagination. His assessment of the stone includes a measuring of his own stature. And as his hand passes over the firm surface his brain is alert, his imagination lit. He is alive.

If the human being is to hold to his identity, he must, somehow or other, keep on making his own discoveries. The tragedy of today is that it is becoming increasingly difficult for him to do so. He is even in danger of becoming a back number, for the powers that would govern his life have found that the machine is, for competitive purposes, so much more efficient and reliable than he is.

When you have lived for a few years in the bare uplands, where life has been precarious from the start, you learn, first, not to panic. Then you are ready to love wholeheartedly what need no longer be feared. You become so deeply involved in the true drama of cherishing life itself that mere attitudes and the pursuit of possessions are discarded as absurd. You discover that under snow there is bread, the secret bread, that sustains.

Panic gone, you can plot a course with steady hand and eye. And, after all, human steadfastness is the only ultimate weapon fit to guarantee survival in a real sense.

That is why I thought it worthwhile to record the process by which three small human beings, completely re-enchanted with their world, found the strength to walk without fear among the astonishing beauty of its wilderness.

I should like to thank Mrs. Anne Shortreed for capturing so delightfully, in line, the spirit of life in the uplands. And my special thanks go to Mr. Neil Gunn, who gave the book his blessing.

KATHARINE STEWART

FOREWORD
to the First Edition
by
NEIL M. GUNN

The typescript of this adventure story reached me out of the blue—or very nearly, for the croft is about a thousand feet above Loch Ness: marginal land, hill-top farming, where on a February morning the blue may be vibrant with lark song or obscured by a snow blizzard. This is the oldest of all Highland adventures and will be the last. It is heartening and heart-breaking. Why do people go on thinking they can make a living out of a hill croft? In particular, what drives strangers, not bred in crofting traditions, to make the attempt? This is the story of such an attempt, with all the questions answered, and it is told so well that I find it absorbing.

For the author and her husband see everything with new eyes. They meet their problems as they arise, and they arise daily. Their capacity for work is all but inexhaustible. If I hesitate to use the word heroic it is because there are no heroics in this human record; only day-to-day doings, the facts of life, but, again, facts that spread over into many dimensions, the extra dimensions that give the book its unusual quality, its brightness and its wisdom. For the attitude to life is positive; it somehow contrives to survive the frustrations; and that today is rare. Often, too, this is seen in coloured threads running through the main texture, as in the growing up of their child to school age and her responses to the myriad influences of the natural scene; or in the spontaneous help given by, and to, neighbours at difficult or critical times—the old communal warmth that survives the hazards, or is there because of them.

I commend this book to all those who are interested in such things and may have sometimes wondered if there is any meaning in the ancient notion of 'a way of life'.

FOREWORD
to the Second Edition
by
EONA MACNICOL

It is a great honour for me to be asked to introduce this reprint of
A Croft in the Hills. The book gave me great delight when first it
appeared, I treasure my copy; and I am happy that now many more
readers may enjoy it too.

I am myself of the old stock of Abriachan, the place which the
author chose for her brave venture into crofting life, I have therefore the keener interest in it. But I know that through this book,
and through the Folk Museum with which she has more recently
been associated, Katharine Stewart has illuminated the crofting life
not only of Abriachan but of the Highlands of Scotland.

CHAPTER I
DIVINE DISCONTENT

WE had both, since our earliest days, found it difficult to live in a city. Every free half-day or week-end, every summer holiday, had found us making for the nearest patch of country, anywhere where we could breathe and smell the earth and see the sky in great stretches, instead of in tiny squares between the huddled roof-tops.

I shall always remember walking down Oxford Street, during a war-time rush-hour, and finding myself nearly losing my footing among the crowd, because my mind's eye was fixed on the rim of a steel-blue Highland loch, and I was smelling the scent of the bog-myrtle and hearing the weird, lonely cry of a drifting curlew. Jim, at that time, used to stand, during the brief spells of leisure his exacting job afforded, gazing through the huge, plate-glass windows of his place of work and seeing, beyond the racketing crowd, an oasis very like the one I had wandered into.

Later, we managed to make some sort of a compromise. We lived on the edge of the country and he went off to work at an unearthly hour of the morning, clad in the respectable black coat and hat of the city worker and shod with large, hobnailed boots (which he changed on arrival), for the two-mile walk to the bus. In the evenings I would go to meet him and in still weather I would hear the ring of the hobnails on the road long before he came in sight.

We had a garden; we had trees and the sky in stretches; we grew vegetables; we kept bees and hens and ducks. But the journeys to and from work were exhausting, though Jim would never admit it, and compromises are never really satisfactory. We were chafing against the tether.

Then Jim's work took him to a small town in the north of Scotland. That was the end; city life is bad enough but small-town life is far worse.

In a city one has, at least, the feeling that there are thousands of kindred spirits about, if one only knew them, folk just as dissatisfied as oneself with the mechanics of living, who know that it is not enough to have acquired some little skill or other, which will enable one to make enough money to buy shelter and clothing and food, so that one may continue to employ one's skill so as to be able to go on buying shelter and clothing and food, and so on... *ad infinitum*. In a city there is at least a spark of the divine discontent, an only half-submerged longing to catch a glimpse of the larger design, but in a small town everyone seems so glad of the boundary wall.

By this time our small daughter, Helen, was growing into a sturdy youngster. As I wandered hand in hand with her, back from the shops and along the row of trim villas to our home, I found my mind straying, as it had done years before in London, to some imagined remoteness.

I pictured Helen splashing in a hill-burn in summer, rolling like a young Sheltie in the snow in winter, racing the wind on the moor, gazing at birds and minute creatures among the grasses. 'Sheer nonsense!' a small, nagging voice would hiss in my ear. 'A child needs all the amenities of town life—a good school and lessons in music and dancing, and all the other benefits civilisation has to offer. Without them she'll only grow into a hopeless misfit.' But... would she? Wouldn't it be better for her to have at least a glimpse of the roots of things, not allow her to accept life as she would a shining parcel neatly wrapped in cellophane? Wouldn't close contact with natural things give her a perspective and a poise she would never lose? I firmly believed it would.

Jim worked long hours; sometimes it was late evening before he reached home, and he would have to leave again in the morning without getting more than a glimpse of Helen. We both knew that it was only half a life we were living.

We had bought, very cheaply, because it was in an appalling state of neglect, a house in a good residential district of the town. We had done it up and found that light paintwork everywhere and the installation of electricity and some additional plumbing transformed it into quite a pleasant place. We tackled the wilderness of a garden and cleared a plot for vegetables. There would be room to keep some hens and even a goat, we decided. We would be able to unearth the beehives we had brought from our southern garden and there were some derelict stable buildings where we thought we could perhaps grow mushrooms.

But there might be objections from the authorities. We still felt hemmed in, particularly as we knew that all our outdoor activities were discreetly observed from behind impeccable net curtains by our distinctly circumspect neighbours! There was no doubt about it, we were getting restless again.

We began to scan the columns of various newspapers, under jobs, houses, houses, jobs. Could we get some sort of a joint post which would allow us to live in open country with security? We made one or two abortive attempts in this direction, and also inspected several smallholdings on the outskirts of the town.

Then we saw it—an advertisement for a seven-roomed house, in a place with an excitingly unfamiliar name, with forty acres of arable land and an outrun on the moor, for the comparatively small sum of five hundred pounds. We got out the map, found the spot and repeated the name out loud, looking wonderingly at each other. Music was sounding in our ears.

Instantly, our minds were made up. It was within quite easy reach; we must see it, just see it, at least.

On Jim's next free day we got out our old van, packed a picnic, opened the map and set off. Through Inverness we went, and along the shore of Loch Ness, to a point about half-way to Drumnadrochit. There, a small road branched off from the main one. There was no sign-post, just this rough-shod track, pointing skywards. 'This is it!' We beamed at each other and put the van sharply at the rise.

We climbed slowly, changing gear every few yards, one eye on the panorama spread out below us, the other on what might emerge round the next blind corner ahead. After about a mile of this tortuous mounting we found ourselves on more or less level ground. Hills rose steeply on either side. There were small fields carved out of the encroaching heather. Croft houses were dotted here and there and there was a school, a tiny post-office and a telephone kiosk.

We made inquiries and found we had another mile or so to go. We came within sight of a small loch, lapping the foot of a shapely hill. It was remarkably like the Oxford Street oasis.

We branched right at this point and the landscape opened out into great distances. Another half-mile and we left the van at the roadside and took, as directed, the footpath through a patch of felled woodland. Then, at last, the roof and chimneys of a dwelling came into view. We stopped at the stile and took a long look at it.

Four-square and very solid it stood, facing just to the east of south, its walls of rough granite and whinstone, its roof of fine blue slate. Beyond it was the steading and in front a line of rowan trees, sure protection against evil spirits, according to Highland lore. A patch of rough grass all round the house was enclosed by a stout netted fence and on either side of the door was a small flower bed.

Round the house and steading was the arable ground and beyond that the moor, rising to the hill-land and to farther and farther hills against the horizon.

It was May and the warmth of the sun was bringing out the scent of the first heath flowers. A small, soft wind out of the west blew on our hands and faces, a bee hummed through the springing grass at our feet. The flanks of the farthest hills were swathed in blue mist.

We saw the good lady of the house. She pointed out the boundaries and we talked of the various possibilities of obtaining a piped water supply. The only well was a good hundred and fifty yards away, and below the level of the house. But she had had a diviner out and her son had started to dig for water at a spot indicated by him, within a stone's throw of the house. We gazed hopefully into this chasm and agreed that it would be all to the good if water could be found there.

The house was in an excellent state of repair; over the lintel was carved the date 1911. We learnt later that the house was actually built in 1910, but as the mason found it easier to make a 1 than a 0 he engraved the date as 1911! We also learnt later that in former times practically every crofter had a trade at his finger-tips, which he practised along with the working of his croft. This house, like nearly all those in the district, had been slated by the man who was to become our nearest, and very dear, neighbour.

Downstairs were two good-sized rooms, one stone-floored, the other with a new floor of wood. The stone-floored room had originally been the kitchen, but as the cooking was now done in a built-on scullery the range had been removed, the original wide hearth restored and a most attractive chimney-piece of rough, local stone built round it. Off this room was a small bedroom and a door leading to the substantial scullery. Upstairs were two good bedrooms and a box-room with a skylight.

Our experience with our town house had taught us what points to look for in examining property. The walls and wood-work were shabby but the structure was sound and weather-proof. It was the sort of house you could start to live in right away.

The steading was of the usual Highland design—a long, low building divided into three parts—byre, stable and barn—with thick stone walls and a roof of corrugated iron, and like the house it was in excellent repair. Beyond it were the ruins of the 'black house' (a small stone cottage, thatched with heather, its walls blackened with peat-reek), which had been the original dwelling on the holding. Opposite the steading, in the shelter of four giant rowans, was a small wooden hen-house.

The fields had been cultivated only spasmodically over the last years, but they had a healthy slope to them, and we knew that it was possible to obtain grants and subsidies for ploughing-up and fertilising such marginal land as this. Only a small area in the one level part of the arable ground was really damp and choked with rushes. We reckoned that a good clearing-out and a repairing of drains would help there. The rough grazing gave promise of a good summer bite for sheep and hardy cattle.

The fencing was patchy, to say the least of it, but we had already noticed on our way through the felled woodland the quantity of quite sound wood that was lying about. Some of it would surely be fit to make into fencing posts, and we knew of an excellent scrap-yard in Inverness where wire could often be picked up very cheaply.

The access road for vehicles was shared by our two immediate neighbours to the east. (In Scotland, as nearly all the glens run roughly east and west, one always goes 'east', or goes 'west', when visiting neighbours.) We could see that deliveries of heavy goods would have to be made during the drier months, as the road surface was distinctly soft, but it seemed to have a reasonably hard bottom and livestock could be loaded at a fank at the side of the main road.

The only thing that did really worry us a little was the lack of shelter. The woodland, which had formerly broken the force of the wind from all the southerly points of the compass, had been felled during and after the war. The view from the scullery window at the back was superb, but there seemed to be little but the heady air between us and Ben Wyvis which lay, like a great, dozing hound, away to the north.

But it was May-time and one of May's most glorious efforts in the way of a day—warm and sweet-scented and domed with milky blue. It is difficult on such a day really to visualise the storm and stress of winter.

We walked to the limit of the little property and stood looking down the strath. Several small, white croft houses stood on either side of the burn flowing down its centre. The fields adjoining them looked tidy and well-cultivated. Plumes of smoke rose from squat chimneys. Here and there were the ruins of former houses, where one holding had been incorporated into another. There was, on the whole, a feeling of quiet snugness about the prospect. It seemed incredible that we were standing nearly a thousand feet above sea-level.

Probably an upland area such as this would never have been settled at all had it not been for the clearances of the eighteenth and nineteenth centuries. One certainly shudders to think of the labour that must have gone into the wresting of the small fields from the bog and heather. The dry-stone dykes remain as memorials to those who heaved the mighty stones out of the plough's way and made the crops sheep- and cattle-proof.

The crofters' tenacity and innate gift for husbandry had resulted in their being able to maintain their families in health in these surroundings. Could we, who had so little experience, reasonably hope to do the same? We had health and strength and a tremendous appetite for this kind of life; we each had close links with the soil. There were Government schemes of assistance undreamt-of by the older generation of crofters and we could realise a certain amount of capital. We were braced and eager to take the leap.

With Helen staggering ahead of us, a bunch of small, bright heath flowers in her hand, we made our way back to the house. I think the lady in possession must have read her fate in our faces. She gave us tea and we told her, as sops to our conscience, that we would think it over and let her know our decision in a day or two.

Quietly and methodically she told us that there was a postal delivery every day, that an all-purpose van called every Wednesday and another on Saturday, but that, as it was often the early hours of Sunday before this latter one arrived, she preferred to deal with the Wednesday one. Small parcels of meat and fish, she said, could be sent through the post.

We made a mental note of all the information she gave us, thanked her and walked slowly back to the road. We *did* have a look at another place on the way home, but it was quite out of the question, twice the price and very inaccessible and, as the French have it, it 'said nothing to us'.

The house on the hill was already making its voice heard. All the way back in the van we listened in silence to what it had to say. It was a supremely honest little place. It hid nothing from us. Its fields had been neglected, its access road was little more than a track, its water supply was altogether unhandy. In winter it was liable to be cut off by impenetrable snow-drifts. But—it offered a challenge. We had enough imagination to visualise its possibilities and most of its impossibilities. Experience had taught us that the worst hardly ever happens, and if it does, it can usually be turned into a best.

Our minds were seething with positive plans. All traces of discontent, however divine, had vanished utterly.

CHAPTER II
THE HOUSE ON THE HILL

Within a week the deed of purchase of the house and land was signed and sealed by us. Occupation was 'to be arranged'. This meant that the seller would be leaving very shortly and that we should take over in the autumn.

Immediately we set about selling our own house. We knew this would not be difficult as it was now classed as a 'desirable residence' and was much sought after, occupying, as it did, a most favoured site in a most favoured neighbourhood. The angels had been on our side after all. Like fools we had rushed to buy it, only wondering by what stroke of luck we had managed to get it so cheaply and easily. Not until after the sale was concluded did we hear the gruesome rumour that the roof was afflicted with dry rot. For several days we were haunted by this nightmare, till a thorough investigation by the builder called in to do the repairs assured us that the rumour was completely ill-founded. There were traces of the activity of woodworm in some of the cupboards but of dry rot there was no sign. So we were able to dispose of our house with the greatest ease and at a considerable profit.

Meantime, we besieged the local offices of the Department of Agriculture and loaded ourselves with pamphlets concerning grants, subsidies and so on. We discovered that we were eligible for a grant of fifty per cent of the cost of an approved scheme of water installation for the house and steading of the croft; that some of the land would qualify for the ploughing-up grant of five pounds an acre and that we could get help with the buying of lime and fertilisers.

We then called at the North of Scotland College of Agriculture, in Inverness, and were told that their expert would come out to take a sample of the soil in the various fields, for analysis, so that the amount of lime needed could be accurately determined, and that he would draw up a complete cropping and stocking programme for us, all this without any sort of fee. Another expert, a lady (later on referred to affectionately as the 'hen wife'), would come to give us advice on all matters relating to poultry-keeping.

Everyone was most friendly and helpful and charming. Helen would sit on my knee during the various interviews and would almost invariably end up with a peppermint to suck or find herself carried off to the typists' room, to be beguiled with bangs on the typewriter, when business was not too pressing! All in all, we felt surrounded by a solid wall of encouragement and goodwill.

Once a week we set off early, to spend a long day at the croft. We cleared rubbish from the outbuildings and repaired the garden fence; we prospected for wells and picnicked on the moor, or in the empty living-room if it was wet. We made the acquaintance of our nearest neighbours and began to get the feel of the place.

About this time, a piece of land to the west of our croft came on the market. It had been bought some years previously by an Inverness man, who meant to run Highland cattle on it. His plans had fallen through and he wanted to dispose of the land. As it would give us some sixty additional acres of good rough grazing, we decided to make an offer for it. So, for ninety pounds, it became ours.

The seller wished, however, to retain the mineral rights. This intrigued us. We made inquiries and discovered that when digging a drain he had come on several deposits of blue clay. He had had an expert from London up to examine these and had been told that they might be of commercial value, but only if found in sufficient quantity to justify excavation. Later on we turned up quite a lot of this blue clay when ploughing our own ground. We sent a specimen to the Geological Department of the Edinburgh Museum and the opinion we received on it tallied with that of the London expert. We are still hoping we may find a use for it some day.

In the meantime this addition to our croft land has provided us, in addition to the grand grazing, with a supply of first-class peat— the black, well-seasoned stuff which cuts into hard, stiff blocks and gives a much hotter fire than the brown, crumbly variety.

Another find on this newly acquired land was the 'golden' well, so called because of the brilliant marsh-marigolds which grow in the boggy ground all round it. This had always been a death-trap for sheep and other animals. On a hungry spring day, irresistibly attracted by the fresh, green growth, they would plunge into the bog for a bite and get engulfed. During our second summer, after we had lost a ewe lamb in this way, Jim cut a channel for the spring overflow and the ground round about is now quite hard and dry. Could a scheme be devised there is enough water in this source to provide a piped supply for all the crofts lower down the strath.

Our search for water near the house had become almost an obsession. We grudged the expense of laying a long pipe-track from the existing well, even though we should have to bear only half of it ourselves. Some further digging in the hole already begun revealed nothing, not even a trickle. We got in touch with another diviner and watched, goggle-eyed with fascination, while the stick jigged and cavorted in his hands. It seemed there was water here, there and everywhere. At last he selected a spot above the level of the house, whence a supply could gravitate easily to a downstairs tank. Our hopes ran high. The digging started but, after three days' heavy work, all that we came on was a thin, muddy trickle which would not pass the analyst's test.

We decided to seek Government approval for a scheme to install a pump at the existing well, which would raise the water to the level of the house. A sample of this water was found to be quite satisfactory and the Department of Agriculture agreed to give us a grant of fifty per cent of the cost of the work.

As the profit on the sale of our town house had been a substantial one, we decided to have some plumbing installed at the croft and to wire the house for electricity. We had been assured that a main supply from the Hydro-Electric Scheme would be available within the next few years. In the meantime the wiring could be connected to a cheap, wind-driven dynamo to provide us with light though not with power.

We looked on this expense as an investment. It would increase the value of the property and it would pay dividends in other ways. Spared the drudgery of incessant water-carrying, we should have more time and energy to give to productive work and I should be able to get quickly through my household chores and be free to take a proper share in the outdoor jobs. The electric wiring we intended to extend to the steading, in part of which we were going to keep hens, on the deep-litter system, with a light to encourage winter egg-production.

It was difficult to find men to tackle the work on the house. Jim was still busy at his job and had only a very limited amount of time and the place was too difficult of access for men to come out daily from Inverness.

Finally we accepted the quite moderate estimates of some young tradesmen, just setting up in business, who would live on the job if we would provide them with the necessaries for camping in the empty house. We gladly agreed and they took up all the bedding, pots, pans, crockery and so on, we could spare, in a lorry, on the day of their preliminary investigation.

There were the usual delays, for material was still difficult to come by. Mid-October came, the time we could spend at the croft grew shorter as the days drew in, and still the main work had not been begun. We were afraid the frosts would set in before the pipe-track was dug.

Jim packed up his job and we decided to move by the first of November. Then the men really got busy. On our last weekly visit we found the place reverberating with hammer-blows and cheerful whistling and shouting and clanking.

The day of our arrival came at last. The removal people had sent too small a van with the result that two journeys had to be made. We had to spend an extra night in town, as it was too late to make the trip ourselves that day.

Next morning, when we reached our destination, we were

greeted by the sight of half our worldly goods standing stacked at the roadside. Furniture, books, pictures, pots and pans stood there, looking forlorn in the chill, grey light.

We had arranged with a neighbour to ferry our belongings from the road to the house on his tractor-trailer, as the van could not manage to make the journey to the house with the access road in its wintry state. Luckily this neighbour had had the good sense to cart all the bedding and really perishable stuff along to the house the day before, and the night had been fine, so no irreparable damage was done.

We changed into gum-boots and started right away to rescue the most precious books, as the sky was clouding and rain threatening. At once we were overwhelmed with goodwill. The tractor came lurching into view and strong arms soon had another load secured. Our eastward neighbour appeared at her door as we passed and offered to take charge of Helen for the day, so that we could get on with the work as quickly as possible. They were already firm friends, she and Helen, and we gladly agreed. On arrival at the house we found a roaring fire in the kitchen, more cheery faces and a welcome brew of tea.

All day the tractor plied back and forth with load after load of goods and chattels. There was hammering and singing and mud and plaster everywhere, but by tea-time we had everything under cover and the beds made up, so we fetched Helen from our kindly neighbour. The men brought pail after pail of water from the well and we all ate an enormous meal of ham and eggs. I even managed to give Helen her tub, as usual, before carrying her through the 'burach' to the safe oasis of her bed. Then we lit a fire in the great hearth in the living-room and sat round it, all six of us, till our eyelids drooped.

Those were happy days as, slowly, our house began to take shape. The men were up at six and had a fire in the kitchen for me to cook breakfast. After dark they worked on by the light of oil-lamps so as to get done and, as they put it, 'out of our road'. Secretly, I think they were missing the pub and the cinema of their little home town. Certainly their singing and whistling grew more light-hearted and obstreperous as they kept up their spirits till the time came for their release. But they were good sorts and did their best in what were, for them, difficult and unusual conditions.

We celebrated Helen's third birthday with a cake I had made weeks before. Our black Labrador presented us with a litter of pedigreed pups. At last the men completed the plumbing and wiring and departed with cheerful waves and 'rather-you-than-me' expressions on their faces.

Then Peter, a young friend of ours who was waiting to start a new job, came to help Jim dig the trench for the water pipe. For nearly three weeks they dug, pausing only for meals and fly cups of tea. Sometimes they would be lost to view in the mist, and only the ring of the pick and the scrape of the shovel told us they were still hard at it. But the job was accomplished, though we were still to wait a long time before the water would flow from the tap.

Meantime, I was clearing rubble from around the outside of the house and making a gravel path to the door so that some, at least, of the mud would not be brought inside on the soles of our boots. I got to know the ways of my new oven and I carried water, and more water!

At last, towards the beginning of December, when the house was more or less straight and Peter had departed, with a twinge of regret, I think, that he had to go back to the city treadmill, we felt we were really settled in. That first evening on our own I went out after dark to get some washing-water from the butt by the back door. I stood, kettle in hand, staring at the sky beyond Ben Wyvis. Great pale beams were moving, like searchlights, across the whole northern section of the heavens. I called to Jim and he stood with me, gazing at these incredibly beautiful northern lights. Then we fetched Helen, wrapped her in a big coat, and held her in our arms, while we all three watched the spectacle. Jim and I felt very small and very humble but young Helen gurgled with delight. At once we joined in her response: this was her inheritance, she had recognised it at once. It was the first of the joys she was to discover in and around the house on the hill.

CHAPTER III
WINTER AND ROUGH WEATHER

As though to put us through a lovers' test our small domain soon took on its most forbidding aspect. We were hardly into December when the first snow came whirling out of the south-west. We woke one morning to find the doors and windows plastered, as though some giant had hurled a vast white pudding at the house.

The first essential was to keep warm. Luckily, we had already got a good stock of logs sawn and split and there were some peats in the barn, left over from the year before, so we could be fairly lavish with fires.

Normally we relied on the kitchen stove for warmth in the daytime and only lit a fire in the living-room in the evening, when we had leisure to sit at it, before bed. But we kept a blaze going in the living-room all that day and, last thing at night, we carried shovelfuls of red embers to the bedroom grate. We put Helen's cot in our room and unearthed all the spare blankets and so spent quite a snug night.

By next morning the road was blocked with snow-drifts, and it was the day the grocer's van was due. Over a steaming cup of morning tea I mentally reviewed the contents of the larder. It was not very promising; we had been caught unawares. Having as yet no sources of supply of our own, we were certainly not equipped to ride out a storm.

The first thing to do was to get water. The pump was not yet connected and, if this weather were to continue, it looked as though the chances of our having water in the tap before spring-time would be fairly remote. Jim took a pail and a shovel and went to dig out the well. Then we thawed out the tap on the water-butt and filled a big crock with washing-water. While I prepared a meal with our last tin of meat, Helen, in snow-suit and gum-boots, went out to revel in her first snow and Jim knocked up a sledge.

In the early afternoon we set off, with Helen perched on the sledge, in search of eggs from a neighbour, half a mile down the road. It was heavy going but we returned home in triumph with all the eggs intact. The sky was pure, deep blue and there was a sparkling silence everywhere. Our little house looked more snug and secure than ever in its winter setting and we felt the bonds that linked us to it grow perceptibly stronger.

Jim brought in more logs while I made an enormous dish of scrambled eggs and then we shut the door reluctantly on the stars and drew the supper-table close to the fire.

All that month winter fretted at us. There was little we could do outside but repair fences between the storms, but we carried several fallen tree-trunks down on our shoulders and cut them with a cross-cut saw. On the fine days we would work away at the chopping and splitting till the sky faded to mauve and clear shades of green and gold came up about the setting sun. Every morning, when I opened the door, I would find two out-wintered Shetland ponies waiting patiently for their bite of bread. They belonged to a distant neighbour and one day we had taken pity on them and given them some crusts. So every morning, till the spring grass came, they would be there to greet us at the door.

In the evenings we made plans and discussed endlessly the absorbing topics of sheep and cattle, hens and pigs, fertilisers and farm-machinery and crops. This 'shop' never grows stale. It has an inexhaustible fascination, perhaps because one has the assurance that one is dealing with fundamentals, perhaps because one knows that there's always the unpredictable lurking in the background ready to upset the best-laid schemes, perhaps just because it relates to things one instinctively loves. We began to long for the days to lengthen and the air to soften so that we could start putting our plans into operation.

On Christmas morning the plumber arrived to try once more to connect the pump. He had walked the two miles from the bus and was quite tired out when he reached us and amazed at the wintry conditions in our hills. In Inverness, he said, there had been promise of a reasonably mild day and he had had hopes of getting the job done. We have now come to accept this sort of thing. We leave home on a bitter winter's morning and find spring, with a flush of green in the trees, at Loch Ness-side. It's not the distance of two miles that does it but the rise of close on a thousand feet. There was little he could do, the plumber decided, so he shared our Christmas dinner and set off again to walk to the bus. At dusk we lit the candles on our little Christmas tree and played games with Helen till bed-time.

There was a party for all the children of the district in the village hall, to which we took Helen. We met her future teacher and a dozen or so lively youngsters. There were games and songs and a piper and there was tea and cakes and oranges and sweets. It was a simple little festivity but a very happy one. Everyone asked kindly how we were faring. 'It can be fearful wild here in the winter', they said, almost apologising for the climate in their hills. 'We like it', we said, and they looked at us out of their clear, shrewd eyes and I think they almost believed us. We began to feel that we nearly belonged.

On New Year's Eve we sat by the fire talking, as usual, and when midnight came we filled our glasses and slipped upstairs and pledged each other over Helen's sleeping head. We went down again and got out the black bun and some extra glasses and put fresh logs on the fire. We thought it more than likely we should have a neighbour for a first-foot. Distance would not daunt the people of Abriachan, we were sure, and the night was fine.

We sat till two o'clock, getting drowsier and drowsier. No one came and we went to bed. At about three-thirty we were dragged from the depths of sleep by what sounded like an aeroplane crashed outside the front door. We fumbled our way into heavy coats and staggered out, to find three neighbours clambering off a tractor. There was much handshaking and back-slapping. We poked the fire into a blaze and drank a toast. Later we helped them to re-mount and stood at the door, watching the tractor lurch off on its way to the next port of call. How the two passengers managed to keep their precarious balance, draped over the rear mudguards, will remain for ever a mystery. But we were immensely cheered by their visit and went back to bed and slept till the middle of the morning.

During the first days of the new year we made many pleasant visits to neighbours. Some we had called on before, but there was one whose house we had never been in. He lived, with his brother and his cousin, in a high fold of the hills to the south-west. Several other families had lived up there at one time, but now only the ruins of their little dwellings are left. Finlay's place, however, had been completely modernised under the Hill Farming Scheme, and there, in the little house nestled in the shelter of the rock, we found a most heartening welcome. We were given tea before a fine red fire and were shown, with quiet pride, the bathroom, the new scullery with its gleaming sink and hot and cold taps, the enamelled cooking stove, the bright paintwork everywhere.

Later we were told how Finlay's forebears had been evicted from a place in a fertile glen and had started all over again in this green upland, first building themselves a rough house of stone and thatch, then clearing little fields from the heather. We were also told how the men who now live there had laboured, as boys, before and after school, to make the road which carries cattle-floats these days up to their snug farmstead. We began to understand how it was that the Highlander made such a splendid pioneer in Canada and New Zealand.

Towards the end of January the wind at last got back to its normal westerly quarter and the air became soft and damp again. The plumber returned and our shining new taps at last began to function. It was thrilling to see the water actually flow from them— it was bright green in colour, but somehow that only added to the delight. After a time the piping settled down till there was only a faint tinge of green about the water and it had no ill effect on our stomachs.

The mild spell, unbelievably, continued. There was almost a warmth in the sun and the midges were dancing. Encouraged by this overture we took a spade to the garden plot. It had been neglected for years, but it had a dry-stone wall protecting it from the north and east and we could see its possibilities. In a couple of days we had the turf skimmed off and our spades bit delightedly into the good, black earth.

We began to get very impatient to start the real work of the place. The first essential, we knew, for the growing of crops, was sound fencing. Every afternoon we went up to the old woodland, selected pieces of timber suitable for making into fencing posts and carried them down on our shoulders. We pointed the ends and stuck them to soak in a pail of creosote.

But we realised that it would take weeks to make all that were needed. Our land marched for almost half a mile with Forestry Commission land. This Forestry land was unfenced, pending replanting, and sheep from various airts were roaming over it and finding their way into our fields. On our next trip to Inverness Jim went to see the Forestry people and asked when they meant to fence. To our astonishment and great satisfaction they said that although they did not intend to plant immediately they would put forward the fencing and make a start at it in the early summer. This news cheered us greatly; it really did look as though things were going our way.

We bought a tractor and a single plough. The tractor had a small bogey attachment and during the long weeks we waited for the ground to dry out for ploughing we found this extremely useful for all sorts of carting work. We were able to fetch wood in large quantities, both for fuel and for fencing posts, and load after load of stones for patching the road.

February brought another blizzard and the road was blocked again, but this time we had the larder well stocked. We were learning! By the end of the month the larks were singing. There is perhaps nothing in hill-life so thrilling as the sight and sound of the first returning lark. You go out, on a still February morning, your footsteps ringing on the hard cobbles of the yard. Suddenly, something makes you stop in your tracks and look up. Against the pale blue sky you see two, maybe three, or even four, small brown specks tossing madly in the air. As you look, one detaches itself from the rest, rises in a series of ecstatic leaps and comes slowly down again, its song rippling from its tiny throat. How something so small can let loose such a volume of sound is what amazes you. Soon the others join it and then the whole sky rings with music.

'The larks are singing!' Each year we make the announcement to one another. The words are sober enough, but what they convey, it is almost impossible to express. It means that our hills and moors are again fit places for new life, for song and work and laughter, all the things we cling to so passionately, in the name of living. Each year, the rising of the larks has meant a little more to us, as we emerge from one more winter to greet the new season.

After the larks come the peewits. They usually arrive at dusk, and far into the darkening we hear their wild crying. Next morning we go out eagerly to watch them flashing and swooping over the bare, brown fields. Each day after that we listen for the curlews and, when we see them gliding over the moor in the evening light and catch the sound of their call, which seems to come from some other very far-off place, we know that spring is really with us.

By mid-March the upper field in front of the house was ready for ploughing. It was to be sown to oats. The bigger field, below the house, was to carry a crop of oats, undersown with grass, and we were to grow two acres of turnips and half an acre of potatoes. Later on we would put more under grass. We were to work on a five-year rotation.

On this still March morning we could feel the warmth of the sun on our hands and faces. Not only to see the sun, but to feel its warmth, that was what gave a lift to the day! Jim hitched the plough to the tractor and began slowly turning over the sward. I stood watching the work from the door and as soon as the household chores were finished I went out to dig the garden. Helen scampered between field and garden, calling encouragement to each of us. It was a morning none of us will forget.

Of course, winter had not finished with us. The very next day, the wind shifted unaccountably to the east and sleet began to fall. Jim finished ploughing the top field, completely unperturbed by the weather, and in the afternoon he made a start at the lower field. We knew that there were patches of bog here and though we had scythed the rushes and given the drain a preliminary clearing the ground was still treacherous. As dusk was falling the tractor stuck and no amount of manoeuvring would get her clear. We went along to our nearest tractor-owning neighbour, who came willingly to the rescue. It was then that we got our first inkling of what good-neighbourliness can mean in lonely places. Since that day, we have borrowed and lent everything from a loaf of bread to a broody hen and have exchanged services of every kind, from a hand at the dipping to the rescue of a snow-bound truck. We are all faced with the same fundamental problems and we have learnt how utterly dependent we are upon one another in dealing with them.

*

CHAPTER IV
CUCKOO-SNOW

WE were soon well in the grip of spring fever. In the lengthening evenings we would take a pleasure stroll round the fields after supper, for to stay indoors had become positively irksome. We acquired our first stock—a dozen laying hens, which we bought from a neighbour. We settled them in the stable, in a litter of peat-moss and straw, and began to keep a tally of eggs laid.

About this time it came to our ears that the croft immediately to our east was likely to come up for sale. The man who had bought it, a few years previously, was trying to run it in the time he could spare from another full-time job and it had become a burden to him. There were about fifteen acres of well-fenced arable ground, some more rough grazing, and the croft carried the right to graze sheep on the open hill on the other side of the road, a right shared by four other places in the neighbourhood. There was an excellent steading, with a brand-new corrugated iron roof, and a small wooden bungalow adjoining it, in place of the ruined dwelling house.

We were tempted to acquire this place as it would give a reasonably good access road to our land. Our own very indifferent road came through part of this holding and in the past, we learned, there had been a certain amount of dispute about rights of way and the upkeep of communal gates and fences. We could grow our first crops in the well-fenced fields, thus giving ourselves time to do the other fencing more or less at leisure. We could winter cattle in the steading and keep the one near home for the house-cow and the hens in deep litter. The proposition was certainly attractive—could we scrape the bottom of the barrel? We had still our basic stock to buy.

For several days we looked at the thing from all angles. Then, over a cup of tea at the kitchen fire, on a blustery, wet afternoon, we discussed it with J. F., the owner of the croft. We could have it lock, stock and barrel, he said, it was proving too irksome for him, with his other commitments. The lock we knew about; of barrel there was no sign! But we agreed to examine the stock. This consisted of one cross cow, in milk (she was brown and horned and had a touch of Guernsey about her, her owner said. This was later borne out by the quality of the cream she produced), and four stirks, all hardy crosses, two score sheep, a couple of goats, two dozen hens, a dozen khaki-Campbell ducks and—Charlie, a straw-coloured Highland pony of uncertain age. There was also a cart, a set of harrows, a mower, a turnip-chopper, barn tools, all things we should need and have to spend precious time looking for in the second-hand market. Here they were on the spot. Finally we did a deal and the signing of one more scrap of paper satisfied our land hunger at last.

The animals were in poor shape and we got them cheaply enough. They had had a lean winter of it, but we knew a summer's grazing could work wonders—and so it proved. We were able to sell the stirks in the autumn for more than twice the amount we paid for them. But in the meantime our immediate problem was to find something to put in their bellies, until such time as the natural herbage had grown sufficiently to satisfy their appetites.

Here, again, our neighbours came to the rescue. Willie Maclean, from over the burn, sent word that we could come at any time to fetch a load of turnips. He was getting on in years and would not be putting down another crop. He had been ill the previous autumn and had only been able to gather in enough turnips to do his one remaining cow. The rest were lying in small covered heaps in the field, and we were welcome to help ourselves to them. We gladly accepted the offer and went round with Charlie and the cart. On our departure we were told 'that was an awful wee load' and we were to 'be sure and come back for another'. As we were about to set off with the second load, we were bidden to come again for some corn sheaves, for 'the horse would be the better of a feed of oats'. On our return next day Sadie, the young girl of the house, was there to help fill the cart with sweet-smelling sheaves and to give a hand to secure the load with stack-rope. We threshed the sheaves in the old-fashioned way, by beating them with a stick, and it warmed our hearts that evening to see the cattle-beasts munching bundles of good oat-straw and chopped turnip and to watch Charlie devouring half a pailful of corn.

We installed Daisy, the cow, in the home byre and cut rushes with a sickle to make her a clean bed. I washed her udder with soap and water and brushed the accumulation of caked mud off her flanks. The College vet. took a sample of her milk for testing and it was declared free of T.B. bacilli. She was a nice quiet milker and we drank quantities of milk from that time on.

We now found ourselves struggling to overtake the rush of spring work. Loads of lime and fertiliser had arrived and were waiting to be spread, there was dung to be carted out to the potato ground, there was still some ploughing to do. We decided we should need some help for a week or two so we asked our good friend the post if he knew of anyone who might be available. There were two brothers, he said, young lads who were often available for odd work. It sounded hopeful.

Next morning Jim went off to see them and a few days later, on a Friday, they turned up for work. They went hard at it all day, carting out lime, while Jim was harrowing with the tractor. On the Saturday they worked with us till evening and we began to feel we were really getting ahead. On Sunday we went for a walk down to Loch Ness-side, in celebration, and found the trees showing a flush of green and the first primroses in flower.

We bought fifty day-old cockerels for fattening and ordered a hundred growing pullets to be delivered in June; these were to be our winter layers.

We now found that the routine work of milking, attending to the poultry and feeding the stirks took up a lot of time, but we managed to keep abreast of the field work and at last, towards the third week in April, we were ready to make our first sowing of corn. The weather had been blustery and uncertain for several days but we felt we couldn't delay any longer. We sowed in the time-honoured way, from a canvas tray slung round the neck. It was satisfying to see Jim pacing up and down, his arms moving rhythmically, the yellow seed-corn falling in a fine arc on to the brown earth. Helen and I were standing, hand-in-hand, at the edge of the field watching him when, over the hill to the east, a great black cloud came sailing. The wind rose suddenly and a moment later snow began to fall. Helen and I had to run for shelter but Jim went calmly on with the sowing. We stood at the kitchen window watching him till he was almost lost to view among the whirling flakes. It seemed to me that there was something symbolic about making one's first sowing in a snow-storm. There must be a riddle in it somewhere, I thought, but I couldn't find the answer.

The black cloud soon passed over and the sky to the west cleared to a limpid green. As I opened the door to Jim we heard the cuckoo call quite distinctly, three times, from the birches on the edge of the woodland. We looked at each other and smiled, A moment later Billy came in, knocking the snow from his boots. 'It's the cuckoo-snow', he said, in his most matter-of-fact voice, and he began calmly washing his hands. We knew then what it was to be bred in these hills. It meant that you took in your stride whatever came, without panic or jubilation: that you foresaw the worst and so were quietly thankful for the best. The cuckoo sang in the snow-storm; the seed was sown. We sat down hungrily to our hot supper.

That was indeed a topsy-turvy spring. No sooner was the sowing of the corn completed than the rain came down in torrents. We stood at the kitchen window in the grey evening light and watched it carving wide runnels in the sloping fields. It looked as though every scrap of seed would be washed clean out of the ground.

The garden plot was now securely fenced and I limed it and put in two dozen cabbage plants. I surveyed the neat rows with some satisfaction, but I had forgotten about the agility of goats. One evening, one of them sailed blithely over the fence and in ten minutes demolished every scrap of young cabbage plant!

We lost almost half the cockerels when a gale blew out the brooder lamp one night. The robber goat died, not from a surfeit of young cabbage, but as a result of the lean winter she had had. We had hoped to use her as a supplementary milk supply, to tide us over the cow's dry period, before calving. But she was a trial, anyway, and as full of tricks as a box of monkeys. It took two to milk her, one to hold her steady and the other to coax the milk into the pail. Daisy the cow, on the other hand, was so quiet and placid that you could milk her in mid-field, without even tethering her.

'April is the cruellest month', I would murmur sometimes, as I watched the sleet lashing the bare ground and saw the thin, dispirited cattle-beasts stand shivering in the lee of the steading walls. But I knew it was only a question of biding our time, of getting used to disappointments and losses. I spent the worst days catching up on arrears of housework, while Jim made fencing posts in the shelter of the barn. We were cheered, too, by visits from neighbours and Helen had many happy games with the children from Woodend and young Bertha, from over the burn. We had first made the acquaintance of this lively, yellow-haired small girl when she had been sent over, one day at the end of winter, with a bottle of milk for Helen, from Willie Maclean's newly calved cow. She had been boarded out with the Macleans since an early age and was one of the many children they had brought up along with their own daughter.

Practically every croft house has one or more of these foster-children and we have seen several grow from little thin-faced waifs into burly youngsters. Their up-bringing is supervised by officials from the city of their birth (in most cases it is Glasgow), who pay them regular visits and provide them with clothing and pocket money. In most cases they are regarded as sons and daughters of the house and they come back, once they are launched into the world, to spend their holidays, or bring their own families to visit in the only real home they have known. In the Macleans' house at this time there was Bertha, aged ten, Billy, twelve and Sadie, eighteen, and they were a happy, lively trio of whom we were to see a lot.

Willie Maclean himself ('Beelack', as the affectionate Gaelic diminutive of his name was pronounced) was a man of the old Highland type, well-read, with an inquiring mind and a genuine courtesy of manner. In his younger days he had been a great piper. His brother was a well-known doctor in Glasgow. His kindly wife would always meet us on the doorstep with the greeting, 'Come away in' and we could be sure of good talk over a cup of tea at her fireside. As we left, her 'haste ye back!' would ring in our ears, as we made our way over the little bridge and along the track through the heather to our home. At night we would see the yellow glow of the light in her kitchen window and in the morning we would watch the smoke rising in a thin blue plume from her chimney and we found it immensely cheering to know we had these hill-folk for friends. They would anticipate our needs before we were fully aware of them ourselves. Many a time Bertha has come flying across the moor with a drench for the cow, because we had mentioned that she was off her feed, or a broody hen to mother some chicks whose own parent had abandoned them.

At last May brought more genial weather. The rush of work was over and we dispensed with the boys' help. Jim borrowed a ridge-plough and ridged the potato field and we spent a couple of days planting potatoes. It is back-breaking work, tramping up and down the drills, bent double, dropping the potatoes into place. But the weather was wonderful and we made a picnic of it. I spread a rug on the grass verge at the top of the field, on which Helen sprawled with her dolls. Every now and again she would seize a small pail of potatoes and thrust a dozen or so tubers solemnly into the ground, then scamper back to the rug and instruct each doll in turn in the art of potato-planting. At mid-day we stretched out on the rug beside her and ate sandwiches and drank flasks of tea. Overhead, the sky was a pale, milky blue and the air rang with lark song. We were glad to be alive and to be doing exactly what we were doing.

With the potatoes safely in the ground there was a lull till turnip-sowing time. We spent most of this gathering fuel from the felled woodland. The Forestry fence was going up rapidly and we wanted to lay in a stock of wood for winter before this useful source of supply was shut off. So, once again, we made a picnic of it and spent several whole days carting loads of wood to a dump on our own ground.

For the turnip-sowing we sought the good offices of Charlie. This was the first field work we had done with him and he at once proved his worth. With the bite of good grass he was now getting he had improved tremendously and was looking almost sleek. No one knew exactly how old he was, but one neighbour reported having seen him working on a croft some miles away nearly thirty years before. But he was by now a firm family friend and we preferred to ignore all rumours about his probable age. He toiled up and down the turnip drills and, quite literally, never put a foot wrong. He was as patient with us novices as an indulgent father, and we found an affection for him which was to grow steadily over the years.

On the first fine, windless day, we sowed the grass seed. It is so light and feathery that even a gentle breeze will scatter it in the wrong direction. We gave the fields a good rolling and felt that at last we could relax a little. There was still much to do, but the pressure had eased.

On the last Saturday in June, when the sun was blazing from a deep blue sky, we packed a picnic and made for Loch Laide. It's less than a mile from our home and it's the perfect place for relaxation; summer or winter, we never tire of walking by its shore. This June day we lay on our backs in the heather, watching a curlew glide round the shoulder of the hill, uttering its long, drowsy call. Then we plunged into the smooth, dark water and Helen splashed in the shallows of the little beach. We made a fire of roots and twigs to boil our kettle; and we walked home deeply refreshed and ready to tackle whatever might come next.

CHAPTER V
FIRST HARVEST

WITH the crops safely in the ground and the cattle and sheep finding a succulent bite in the clean, natural grazing, we had time to take stock of our position and to analyse rather more closely our aims, both long-term and immediate. Our farming, even bolstered as it was by Government subsidies, could never be more than subsistence farming: we were fully aware of that. As a business proposition its appeal was absolutely nil, but, of course, we had never looked at it—in fact, we had never looked at anything—strictly in that light. As a way of life it had endless fascination and reward—the smallest thing could give us a glow of satisfaction. To see the green flush of corn shoots, or of turnip seedlings in ground that had yielded nothing for years, was an obvious thrill. But there were also the small delights of watching a drain flow freely after it had been cleared of silt, of driving the horse and cart along a road made passable with new patchings of stone, of seeing the sheeps' foraging among the new-sown grass thwarted by a stout fence, hung on the posts we had made in the dark, winter days. Every way we looked there was a reward and a new challenge springing up behind it, something to give us a small, encouraging pat on the back and to spur us on before we had time to smirk.

Perhaps one of the greatest satisfactions of our life was the knowledge that we were in this thing together, as a family, as a unit. There was no seeing father off every morning, to struggle with his own remote set of problems, while mother and child coped with theirs at home. There were no watertight compartments. When it was time to hoe the turnips we all set off to the field together and worked side by side all day, Helen, too, wielding a diminutive hoe among the seedlings. At supper-time Jim stoked the fire and, when we'd eaten, we tackled the day's accumulation of dirty dishes together and it took only a few minutes to smooth the well-aired beds before we slipped between the sheets!

Good food we had in abundance: not for us was the policy of selling every available egg to the van and buying doubtful commodities in their place. It was surely better, we felt, to have a huge, golden-shelled egg on your breakfast plate and health in your eye, than cash accumulating in the tin box. Likewise with milk—though there, of course, there was no question of any being sold—the best was for ourselves. The rich, yellow cream we would churn into butter, after setting aside the jugfuls for porridge and tea. Any surplus would be fed to the growing chickens. Later on we hoped to rear a baconer for our own use and some table poultry.

When the garden really came into production we meant to have a good supply of all the hardy vegetables and fruit. An evening stroll with the gun would often yield a couple of young rabbits for the pot. Very good they were in those days, and now, although the crops are certainly better off without them, we do miss the meals they gave us.

In fact, our aim was to be as far as possible self-sufficient in the way of food and to cut down other living costs to a minimum. The fuel problem, for instance, we hoped would take care of itself, with the limitless supplies of peat and dead wood that were to hand. As for clothes, they had only to be serviceable, not decorative, so that hard-wearing stuff such as corduroy and denim and leather, which would survive for years, was our chief rig. In Helen's case, of course, we had to allow for growth, which was rapid. But, by buying things several sizes too big and taking in ample reefs and tucks, even these were made to last. Corduroy slacks, which began voluminous and ankle-length, she could still wear several years later, almost skin-tight and reaching not much below her knees, and still be in the fashion! Only on footwear were we all extremely hard, and gum-boots and leather shoes have had to be renewed at alarmingly frequent intervals.

The surplus eggs were already beginning to bring us in a useful supply of ready cash, and in an extremely handy way. Every Thursday we left a boxful at the gate for collection by the van from the packing-station and the following Thursday we found an envelope containing the pounds, shillings and pence and a note explaining exactly how many eggs were first-grade, second-grade, cracked or 'rejects'—so that we knew where we were and what we could count on in this department. The grocer's van was calling regularly every week and the money from the previous week's eggs usually met his bill for bread, tea, sugar, butcher-meat and oddments.

In other ways, too, we meant to be self-sufficient. We had to rely on our own resources for mental stimulus. We had hundreds of books, accumulated over the years, and we had come to treat them with a new respect during the evenings of our first winter in the hills. We had always read a lot and loved music. But to read a book in a half-circle of firelight, with the feet-deep snow outside cutting off all possible interruption, to hear on the wireless a symphony of Sibelius above the shrieking of a north-east gale, is to experience these things in the raw. I shall always remember rereading *Wuthering Heights* in these conditions and entering, as it were, barefoot, into Emily Brontë's world.

The last thing we wanted to do was to run away from life. We were all too well aware of what went on in the wider world and we listened as avidly as the next household to B.B.C. news bulletins and talks on current affairs. We could get a paper delivered to the door on the afternoon of its day of publication. But we did firmly and passionately believe that close contact with natural things was the only means of getting the savour of balanced living. It was the deeper world we wanted to explore, not the wider.

On the croft we could work hard all day, feel the sun on our hands or the rain on our faces, come in to eat food fresh from the ground and still have time to stand on the doorstep in the evening light, to watch the birds gliding in the shadowed air, engaged in their own lives, and to see the stars come out, and to wonder.

We were fully aware of the fact that man had prefabricated a ghastly doom for himself. Nuclear weapons could destroy cities, could wipe out the records of a whole civilisation, and that was bad enough. But that they could also destroy the earth upon which, ultimately, all depended, that was the final horror, we felt. To devote all one's energy to working for the banning of the use of nuclear power as a weapon, was that the only reasonable thing to do with one's life, we sometimes wondered. But negative purposes have never a deep appeal. Surely the only appropriate gesture to make in the face of enormity is a positive one, however small. We could cultivate our portion of earth. It was little more than wilderness, lying exposed to every kind of blasting weather, but it was earth, and earth responds. Learn to understand it a little, work along the rhythm of it and it will repay you in ways beyond your reckoning.

Soon we saw a thick green sheen come over the cornfields and the potatoes began to push through in crowded rows. The garden plot, which had been so well limed and manured, was producing lettuces of real succulence and flavour.

The stirks were coming on amazingly well on the natural grazing and were scarcely recognisable as the lean, shivering creatures we had bought only two or three months before. Our aim was to sell them profitably in the autumn and buy in a couple of good calving heifers, from which we would build up a small herd of four or five breeding cows. There were two licensed Aberdeen-Angus bulls in the district, for service. The sheep also we meant to sell at a profitable time and with the proceeds buy a score or so of well-bred, black-faced ewes or gimmers, to form the nucleus of a breeding flock which we could increase to about a hundred.

We meant to keep a hundred and possibly, later on, two hundred pullets in deep litter and to rear a few pigs if feeding permitted. Our plan was to slough off all the rag-tail stock by the autumn and start afresh then. And so it worked out.

The first item in the new stock we had to acquire almost at once—a hundred five-week-old pullets, which were to come into lay about the end of September. We put them into two rearing houses in a field near the house and let them run on good clean grass. All went well until the weather broke but then the trouble started. Almost every morning we would bring in two or three sodden chicks and dry them out in boxes by the stove. As they grew bigger they began to crush each other on cold nights and we would retrieve one or two small suffocated bodies from the pile in each corner of the hen-house. We tried every device to keep them from crowding, but to no purpose. They were obstinate little devils and seemingly had entered into a vast, grisly suicide pact. By the time they developed some sort of sense we had lost at least twenty of them, and even then our patience nearly gave out, as we dodged each other round the henhouses each evening at dusk, chasing the elusive little rascals in to bed. The two or three ex-broody hens, who were complacently rearing ducklings in the next field, looked on at these manoeuvres with a faintly derisive twinkle in their elderly eyes. Don't you know there is no substitute for mother, even foster-mother, love, they seemed to say!

We had no hay crop to worry about that first summer, and once the turnips were hoed and the potatoes ridged we turned the attack once more to the ever-recurring problem of fencing. Our southern flank was now very adequately protected by a first-class Forestry Commission fence. To the north and east we were moderately well defended but our western approaches were badly in need of safeguard. We had a frontage here of three or four hundred yards along the roadside and the fence was practically non-existent. So, one Saturday, we loaded the trailer with posts and wire, packed a picnic basket and set off for what we called 'the west end'.

We had had a spell of very dry weather and the water was coming into the storage tank in the house in only the smallest of trickles so we had to use it very sparingly indeed. At the 'west end' there is a burn which never dries up. It has its source in the hill and its water is clear amber and lies in pools, where the small trout flash. Remembering this burn, and the cool delight of it, I packed a bundle of washing and a bar of soap among the fencing material and, while Jim dug holes for the strainers, I did the family wash in a pool of golden water. I hung it to bleach on the dwarf alder bushes, while Helen splashed about and floated twig boats in the pool. We made a fire to boil our tea kettle and afterwards I helped to stretch wire for Jim. We bumped home happily in the trailer, Helen and I each clutching a bundle of clean linen, Jim whistling softly with satisfaction at the thought of a job well begun.

We spent several more days working at that fence. Strangers passing along the road in cars, seeing our picnic fire and Helen gallivanting in her sun-suit, mistook us for holiday-makers and gave us an encouraging wave. We waved back enthusiastically for we did almost feel we were on holiday. I say almost, because even the most fascinating of holidays had never given us quite as satisfying a feel as most of our working days gave us. To know you were achieving something real, in the best company in the world, with the sun warm on your hands and all the wild things you loved—bird, hill, flower, sky—surrounding you, was deeply pleasurable. Of course, we hammered our thumbs, we dropped staples at crucial moments in the rushes, we tore our legs on pieces of barbed wire, but that was just the pepper and salt. When the last stob was in and the last wire tightened, we waded in the burn with Helen and sat on the bank watching a heron flap his lonely way up to the lochan in the hill beyond Rhivoulich.

By the third week in September the corn was ripe. This is a reasonably early date for these heights—the previous autumn we had seen stooks still lying out in November. And the crop was really one to be proud of. We had had a very heavy thunderstorm in August which had laid part of the oats in one field, where the yield was particularly heavy. But, on the whole, it was a good, standing crop. On the twenty-fourth of the month Jim began cutting 'roads' for the binder, that is, cutting a border around the edge of each field with a scythe to allow the binder to work freely without damaging any of the corn. I followed in his wake, tying the swathes into bundles with a stalk and setting them up in stooks.

We hadn't been long on the job when we saw Willie Maclean making his way slowly across the burn and up through the heather to join us. He was leaning heavily on his stick and he looked tired and a little shaky, but his face lit with pleasure as he picked up a sheaf and shook it by his ear. 'It rattles!' He beamed at us through his glasses, 'It's fine when you hear it rattle!' He looked over the small golden field appraisingly. 'It's a grand crop you have there', he said, and we felt a small glow of pride. To hear a neighbour praise a crop or a beast always brings a small thrill of pleasure to their owner. Hill people are not given to expressing enthusiasms, but when they do, in their own quiet, well-worn phrases, you know you can believe what they say.

In a couple of days the corn was cut and then began the laborious process of stooking. Everyone was busy at the same time, with their own crop, so that it was impossible to exchange help. But the weather remained magnificent until the last afternoon. It was a Saturday and we began to panic just a little as we saw the sky clouding and felt the first small drops of rain. We had to get the field in stook before dark so we worked on steadily, stopping only for a snatched cup of tea and then, at about half-past four, we saw a pair of legs swinging over the fence at the top of the field. Their owner gave no sign that he'd seen us working away at the bottom, but simply began stooking his way in our direction. Only when we were within earshot did he greet us with 'Aye, aye, you'll be wanting to get done before the rain'. It was our friend Bill (pronounced Beel) the post. He'd finished his letter-round, his own well-nursed crop was already in the stook and he'd arrived exactly at the right time to give us the lift we needed.

For several weeks the crop stayed out in the stook. Then one afternoon, Alec, an easterly neighbour, and his two boys arrived, unannounced, in the field. He stood looking round the crop. 'It would be as well in the rick, I think', he said, as he pulled a handful of grain from the nearest stook and straightaway he and the boys began stacking the sheaves into a small circle. A short while later Willie Maclean appeared, with Billy and Bertha in his wake, and the nine of us worked with gusto.

It was a perfect October evening. The sky was glowing red and the air was pungent, with a hint of frost. When the enormous yellow moon came looming over the arc of the hill, I went up to the house with Helen and Bertha and we stoked the fire, to set the kettle boiling, and made toast and a panful of fried eggs.

On the next two evenings this band of neighbours worked with us, till all three cornfields were decked with small, sturdy ricks. 'It'll be safe enough now, whatever', they said, as they bade us good night. They had quietly watched our progress through the year and had taken, I think, a modest, communal pride in our first harvest. They just wanted to be sure we should secure it, knowing as they did from their long experience what tricks the weather was capable of. We marvelled at their undemonstrative good-neighbourliness, and we blessed them for it.

Later on we had a couple of days' hired help to make the big stacks, from which the corn would be threshed. The last few ricks had small caps of snow on them before they were at last brought in. When the stacks were completed, on the last day of October, we knew what had gone into the fashioning of them—the work, the anxiety, sunshine, storm, good fellowship—the whole of our new life was symbolised in those five rugged cones, standing stark against the crackling stars.

Yes, it was the last day of October when we put aside our pitchforks, and we'd hardly had time to eat supper and warm our stiff, calloused fingers at the fire, when there was a loud knock at the door and into the kitchen marched the oddest-looking collection of creatures we'd ever seen. Their faces were completely masked in old bits of black stocking, or white calico. On their heads they wore scooped-out turnips, battered hats or turbanned scarves. The remaining parts of their persons were swathed in garments that defy description; one wore a horse-hair tail. We'd almost forgotten —it was Hallowe'en, and these were the guisers. After various attempts to guess their identity had failed, we offered them apples and sweets, which they had the utmost difficulty in eating, as their mouths and even their hands were muffled in disguise. However, an ill-suppressed giggle finally revealed the identity of one or two of them and they were persuaded to sing a song for a sixpence before they disappeared into the night.

The stacks became so much a part of the landscape that we were quite sorry to see the arrival of the threshing-mill and to have to undertake the slow dismantling of them. However, there was compensation in watching the plump, burnished grain pouring out of the hoppers into the sacks and to note that there was an astonishing amount of first-grade stuff among it. We would take a sample in a grimy palm and gloat over it, like a miser with his gold.

Our corn had been sown in a snow-storm and it was to see another before it was finally gathered in. When the job was three-quarters done the snow began to fall in soft, feathery flakes. It was not wetting stuff and did not deter the squad. But next day, when Billy came to help us finish off the straw-stack, it was blowing a blizzard and most of the chaff, which I had looked forward to gathering for the deep-litter house, was soaked. However, the grain was got safely under cover and Jim and Billy battled away with the stack of straw and secured it with weighted ropes. Next day, the seed-merchant's lorry came to collect the surplus grain and we received a substantial cheque.

Billy worked with us for several days, clearing up the aftermath of the threshing, and we decided to get him to stay on for a bit at a weekly wage. We had the potatoes to riddle and the turnips to lift and we foresaw winter catching up with us before this work was done, if we had no help. A bothy was fitted up for Billy in the bungalow and he had food with us in the house.

We borrowed a mechanical riddle and sorted the potatoes into ware, seed and chat. We found we had several tons surplus to our own needs, which we sold at once rather than risk having them deteriorate in the pit.

We sold the sheep and the stot stirks, keeping the two heifer stirks, one black and one blue-grey, which had improved sufficiently to warrant retaining, and bought thirty-five magnificent black-faced ewes and a ram, the sort of beasts any sheep-man would be proud to own.

Finlay, from up the hill, had given us a collie pup, Bess, and the place began to echo with shouts and whistling, as we started to train her to the shepherding. She was so anxious for work that she would be for ever rounding up whatever came in sight—hen, pullet, duck, cow, or anything else.

We were well into winter by the time the last of the turnips was lifted and pitted. The pullets were snug in their deep-litter house, the cow and the heifers were warmly bedded in straw, Charlie was crunching oats in his stable. With our first harvest secured, we could face the coming months with a reasonable measure of confidence.

CHAPTER VI
CEILIDHS

Two days after Christmas, the day of the little children's party we had planned, the ram died. He had been ailing for a week or so and we had done our best in the way of dosing, but to no purpose. As I looked up from my sandwich-cutting, at the kitchen window, I saw Billy making his way slowly up through the rushes in the lower field, carrying the bedraggled hulk of the once majestic creature on his shoulders. It was a sad moment, but luckily we hadn't time to brood. Jim and Billy performed the brief funeral rites, while I brought out the jellies and cream.

Eight youngsters from the three neighbouring crofts arrived at dusk, their faces gleaming with cleanliness and anticipation, and we had a very lively party indeed, Billy joining in with surprising gusto. The children taught us their own enchanting singing games, which have since become our favourites—'The wind and the wind and the wind blows high' and 'We are all maidens' and 'In and out the dusty bluebells' and many others with sweet, nostalgic cadences. Party-making is easy when you have unlimited quantities of eggs and cream, one of the little self-sown conifers (which need thinning, anyway) for a tree and a handful of unspoilt youngsters, eager for enjoyment. Each year we have a small gathering of children in the house at Christmas. Soon after Hallowe'en we start planning it and long after it's over it's still a subject of chuckling reminiscence.

The smallest social occasion has a savour to it here. Some neighbours we may only see twice, or at most three times, in a year. They live, perhaps, only a mile or so away, but in the summer they're busy with their crops and in the winter snow or storm may prevent them venturing far at night. So, when we do meet, it's a small celebration in itself. First comes the firm handshake, as we congratulate each other tacitly on the fact that we are still in the land of the living. Then come the comments on the state of the weather and on the condition of crops and beasts, leading to the climax of the interview—the exchanging of any real tit-bits of news, the spicier the better! Finally, over a cup of tea, or a dram, if it is a really special occasion, a mellow, reminiscent mood settles on the company. This is when Jim and I hold our breath and wait for the old stories to come out for an airing in the fireside glow. We hear of an old bachelor who lived in the remains of a once-model croft house and would tether his cow to the foot of his bed to keep her from straying at night: of Mary, who had the second sight, and could see, on a winter evening's walk, the funeral procession of those who were soon to die: of the old widow who had the evil eye and could bring about the death of a favourite beast, or wish ill-luck on a whole family. These were all men and women who had lived hard lives, had been a law unto themselves and had left their legend lurking among the tumbled stones which had been home to them.

We never pass one of these pathetic ruins but we visualise the children scampering about the doorways. Many of them died young, as the headstones in the burial ground testify, but most of those who survived left their mark in other parts, in Canada or New Zealand. The depression in agriculture after the First World War was the immediate cause of many of these upland holdings being abandoned, but probably it would have come about in any case. With the improvement in communications, the standard of life was changing: the community was no longer isolated. The young people could get to town at the cost of a two-mile walk to the bus, instead of having to wait for the odd occasion, when they would go on foot, or on the steamer on Loch Ness. Once in town they would fall under the spell of the shop-window. A small holding could not stand the strain of providing cash for bought commodities. When the old diet of milk, meal, potatoes, eggs and a barrel of salt herring, carted from the west, was no longer considered adequate, holdings had to be enlarged or other means of subsistence found. Whether the children are healthier now, with the addition of tea and wrapped bread and sweetstuff to their menu, is perhaps a moot point. Certainly, preventive and remedial health measures save them from the epidemics which carried off many youngsters in the old days. These epidemics, when they did occur, hit them exceptionally hard, reared, as they were, in isolation from germs, and so lacking natural immunity. Labour-saving devices do spare the women, and the men, a lot of killing drudgery. But how far the real quality of human health and happiness has been improved would be difficult to say. To look at the serene faces and hardy frames of some of the older generation is to make one doubtful of using the word 'improve' at all. One neighbour it is always a special delight to meet is a grandmother of close on eighty who lives, now, alone in her croft house. She has reared a large family and has known every kind of trouble and grief. Yet there is always a smile on her face, to challenge the wrinkles; and she thinks nothing of walking miles, straight across country, fording burns and climbing fences, to visit relatives of a younger generation who may be sick.

Finlay, who guided us in all our affairs with sheep, on hearing that the ram had died, immediately gave us one of his on loan till the end of the tupping season. So our fear that some of the ewes might not bear lambs was allayed.

The year came to an end with a storm of alarming fury. The scullery window was blown right out. One of the henhouses (mercifully devoid of hens) was scattered in bits across the field. But, miraculously, the straw-stack stood intact: we blessed the day we had battened it down with weighted ropes. After battling with the elements in the kitchen, doing my indoor chores in gum-boots and balaclava, I developed a heavy cold and we spent our Hogmanay dozing over a huge fire, myself well drugged with aspirin.

New Year started auspiciously for me, with Jim and Helen bringing me tea and toast to bed, and immediately all sneezing and snuffling were at an end! In the afternoon we walked out across the moor in the still, glittering cold and came home to a dinner of roast duck.

Then the ceilidhs began. Since the previous Hogmanay our neighbours had become friends and a good year's work had established a firm bond among us. We knew our way about. To us there is no place on earth so comforting as a croft kitchen on a winter night. As you approach the glow of the lighted window, the smell of the peat-reek comes at you in a waft of welcome, pungent and homely. On reaching the threshold you brush the snow from your boots with the small besom provided for the purpose. Then the door opens and you're bidden, with an outstretched hand, to 'come away in'. Inside, the flames are licking round the up-ended peats, there's the hiss of the pressure lamp and the ticking of a huge, old clock. The pattern is the same everywhere. It hardly varies, yet it never fails to delight. We're a little company gathered in sheltering walls that huddle against the vastness of the night and of the cold. We're supremely glad to have warmth and calm and relaxation.

The men stretch their legs and slowly stuff their pipes. The women move quietly about, placing the kettle, the tea-caddy, the cups in strategic positions. The children sit, bright-eyed, on the settle, hoping bed-time will be overlooked: at New Year, it usually is. The kettle is not brought to the boil till the men have had their dram, the women their glass of port and the children their fruit wine, to wash down the raisin-cake and shortbread. Tongues are loosened at this time of year and throats well moistened. You can almost forget the wireless in the corner by the window, the weekly paper stuffed under the chair cushions, and expect the ceilidh to resume its old character. You almost wait for the song and the story to come floating out of the shadowy corners of the room, but of course they don't. The stories are reminiscences, fascinating in themselves and never wearisome, however often they are repeated. They're founded on fact and they haven't the wild sweep and gusto of the old, imagined tales. The song, too, has died. There is no longer even the cheerful scrape of a fiddle, though here and there a young lad will produce a tune from an accordion 'box'.

We spent many evenings at neighbouring firesides that New Year. Helen enjoyed them as much as we did and was indulged with sweets and oranges, and walked home across the moor at midnight without a stumble, scorning to be carried.

The days were not arduous, for there was little we could do but feed the horse, the cattle and the hens, look over the sheep and split logs for the fire. Jim and Billy did, however, get ahead with the fencing, whenever the weather allowed, and made several gates. I tackled the accumulation of mending and took advantage of the well-banked state of the fire to do some large bakings.

On the worst days, when all outdoor work was at a standstill and it was too cold even to work in the barn for more than an hour or two together, we all turned our attention to improving the living arrangements in the house. All through the previous year we had used only the ground-floor rooms, for warmth in the winter and for convenience in the summer.

Now, however, we began to explore the possibilities of the upper regions. I scrubbed out the two bedrooms and the men shouldered the beds and furniture up the narrow stairway. The walls and paintwork were shabby in the extreme, but decorating would have to wait until the better weather came. The rooms were clean and we installed an oil-stove in each, which we would light an hour or so before bed-time each night.

Then we made the spare downstairs room into a second sitting-room, where we could relax, or so we hoped! The living-room had a felt-and-linoleum covering over the stone and we could go in there gum-booted, dogs at our heels, without fear of doing damage. The new sitting-room we planned as a sort of inner refuge, snugly carpeted, its walls lined with the books and pictures we had at last extricated from the boxes in the cupboard. Outdoor footgear and dogs were to be strictly prohibited. We foresaw long Sunday afternoons spent in the comfort of this oasis, but actually it didn't turn out that way. Sunday afternoons were usually spent attending to lambing ewes, chasing cattle out of the crops or catching up on domestic work, and the room itself had often to be converted into sleeping quarters for a benighted contractor. But still, we did enjoy brief moments in it and the knowledge that it was there was a satisfaction in itself. We began to feel we had got past the stage of the initial assault and were beginning to dig in for the campaign.

It was not a hard winter and by mid-February the larks were singing. Soon, we began to sense the slow tilting of the earth towards the sun and then a rash of activity broke out. Dung was carted to the fields, the vegetable plot was enlarged and dug, houses were got ready for the new batches of chickens.

We got wind of activities on other fronts. The hill-road down to Loch Ness-side was being widened and resurfaced, the worst of the bends rounded and a fine new bridge built, to replace the rickety one over the burn that cascaded down from Loch Laide. It was said that when this work was completed, the bus company would seriously consider putting on a weekly service to Inverness.

There were rumours of various new enterprises starting up in the district. A nursery garden, at the foot of the hill, where tomatoes were grown in soil heated by electricity generated by local water-power, was already well established. Now, we learnt, another 'in-comer' was to cultivate the sheltered slopes immediately above this garden for the production of soft fruit: another was setting up a small dairy farm and yet another was going in for mink. The place was buzzing with reports of the activities of the 'tomato-man', the 'strawberry-man', the 'mink-man' and the 'dairyman'. All these concerns were sited in the comparatively sheltered district overlooking Loch Ness. Each time we passed that way on our journey to town we would watch, goggle-eyed, for signs of the progress of these fascinating enterprises. We began to feel, with our adoption of more or less traditional methods, distinctly back numbers. Still, our oats had impressed even the seed-merchant the previous autumn and our ewes were in grand shape. Perhaps there was something to be said for a quiet merging into the landscape.

The scheme for the testing of cattle came into operation at this time. We had ours tested and found, to our dismay, that Daisy and one of the heifers were reactors. Daisy's milk had been declared free of bacilli and she appeared to be in radiant health, but she didn't make the grade, so she and the heifer had to be despatched to the market at once. We bought in a good cross cow, brown, with a white star on her forehead, which we christened Hope, in token of our feeling towards her, and a sleek, demure, quite enchanting little cross-Shorthorn heifer, which we could only call Pet. The name exactly fitted her.

The byre had a thorough cleansing and disinfecting and whitewashing before these new beasts were installed in it and we hoped our little herd could now be established without further skirmishings. A cow, particularly a house-cow, is so much a part of the family that one hates to have to exchange her for another. We had just got to know all Daisy's little whims and quirks, knew what blandishments she particularly appreciated and how to humour her and to cope with her occasional moods. Now we should have to start all over again with Hope. She was to calve in a few weeks' time and was slow on the move and quite placid; she proved an excellent milker and we soon came to have a real affection for her. A cow certainly responds to kindness. I soon discovered that Hope would let down her milk most willingly to music—'Lilli Marlene' was her favourite tune. As soon as I began to intone it, to a slow rather melancholy rhythm, I would glance along her back and see her ears twitch and a dreamy look come into the one eye visible to me. Then the milk would spurt steadily into the pail and I knew all was well.

The pace of spring was now increasing rapidly. Each evening at dusk we would see the gleam of fires, as the heather was burnt to make room for new growth. In the distance we could see the small black specks of figures silhouetted against the glow. With sticks and switches they were keeping the flames under control. The boys of the neighbourhood took a sort of primitive delight in assisting at these firing operations, and it did seem as though the purifying flames were really laying the ghost of winter in the hills.

With the approach of the lambing season there was another ghost to be laid—that of the threatening, elusive fox. A drive was organised and all guns mobilised. One cold Saturday afternoon Jim and Billy set off, with the others, to search the crags and thickets round the Red Rock. They swarmed up precipices and slid down scree, but never a fox did they bag. However, a gesture had been made and some good sport enjoyed. Communal activity always acts as a tonic—the men came home with a gleam in their eyes and a chuckle in their throats.

The ploughing was easier that year, for Jim and Billy could take turns at it, and all the field work went quite smoothly. But we were coming to a crucial point in our enterprise. Our capital was all laid out in the land and stock and it would be some time before either could give us a substantial return. Could we hold on and keep the place going till that time arrived? Were we justified in paying Billy a wage, small though it was? As Jim crawled up and down the field on the tractor, as I gathered pailfuls of stones from the garden plot, with Helen making mud pies in her own corner, these questions were nagging away at our minds.

Finally, we went to see our man of business in Inverness. He is at all times most helpful and understanding, and a problem shared is usually half-way to being solved. The banker, too, was co-operative. All bankers have a spine-chilling effect on us, but I think the small country-town banker who, in many cases, is of farming stock himself, is perhaps the one representative of the order who does come within our understanding. Our particular banker has enjoyed several days shooting grouse and hares over our acres and looks positively human in rough tweeds with a gun under his arm.

Finally, we decided that we could cope with the situation and that Billy could be kept on for the time being at any rate. The pullets were showing a profit and at this peak time of egg production we would be cleaning eggs till midnight, while listening to a radio play. The ducks, too, were laying again. The sun had a warmth to it, coltsfoot was blazing along the sheltered bank of the burn, the peewits were tossing and flashing over the fields, the wild geese had gone off, honking their way gaily into the white north sky. It was a time of promise after all.

Hope presented us with a tidy little black bull-calf, one morning at seven. Two days later the first of the lambs was born. Each morning after that we would look out first thing to see how many new white specks had appeared on the moor overnight. Helen was the quickest at spotting them and she kept the tally. Each evening we would walk right round the flock, watching for any ewe that needed help; but they were wonderful mothers and we only lost one lamb. Billy quickly skinned it and draped the small, fleecy coat over the body of a lamb which had lost its mother. The bereft ewe, after an astonished nosing, adopted it as her own. We had some anxious moments, for there are so many creatures ready to make a meal of a new-born lamb—the fox, the buzzard, the killer dog. The weather itself can be cruel. Driving rain is one of their worst enemies. But we were lucky, for the weather though cold was mostly dry, and the lambs got safely on their feet and began to thrive.

One Sunday in mid-April, when everything was more or less under control, we left Billy in charge and set off for Loch Ness-side. The primroses were in flower on the wooded slopes, the birds were singing their heads off in the leafing trees. The water was blue and glittered in the sunlight. It was a morning out of time and we each had a foot in Eden.

CHAPTER VII
THE PIGLETS ARRIVE

By the end of April the place was swarming with young things. Hope's calf was let out of the byre and went charging round the field like some fantastic clockwork creature. Home-hatched ducklings were weaving through the rushes, in a long, golden line. Tiny yellow balls of chickens were scattered over the short, bright grass. Lambs, startlingly white, as though freshly laundered in a favoured brand of detergent, were bouncing about in the heather and making wild dashes across the fields. Then the goat made a contribution to this nursery world, in the shape of a tiny brown kid. It was the most fascinating baby creature of them all. Faun-like, yet quite fearless, with bright, intelligent eyes, it would stand poised on a pinnacle of stone, gazing quizzically at everything, then suddenly leap and cavort in the air, for the sheer joy of using its limbs. Helen would watch its antics for hours on end, completely under its spell.

Meanwhile we had, thanks to our banker, added a further twenty gimmers to our sheep stock and put a fresh batch of five-week-old pullets in the rearing-houses.

We certainly had our hands full, but it was a real delight to be working among all these young things. We didn't find the long hours a burden. I think the spring air, the fresh, plain food and the deep, trance-like sleep we fell into at night kept us going. This sort of life generates its own energy, it imposes its rhythm and if you respond to it you can keep up a steady pace. There is none of the rushing and jolting, interspersed with blank spaces of boredom, which wastes so much vital force in an artificial way of living. It has its own routine, of course, but within that routine there is always something fresh cropping up to hold the interest and to challenge initiative powers. One is conscious of keeping all the faculties in trim—brain, brawn, imagination and understanding are all constantly in play. One is on one's toes, yet relaxed.

There was now only one thing needed to complete our happiness—a pig! Could we woo the banker to the point of allowing our overdraft the generosity to embrace one little porker, we wondered. It appeared we could. Anyhow, Jim went to Dingwall market one beautiful May morning and came home with, not one pig but four small, squirming bundles of sacking in the back of the van, and a triumphant twinkle in his eye. As we loosed each bundle its contents turned out to be a plump, dapper little porker, which scampered round the pen then stood four-square in front of us, on its neat, pink trotters, looking at us out of unwinking eyes, brashly demanding sustenance.

We had to like the little beggars. They were impudent, yet fetching and they grew at an alarming rate. We had skim milk for them and potatoes, to which we added protein, and they found a lot of nourishment in the ground itself. In fact, we had always wanted a pig or two, not only because the market was good and they could give a quick return, but also because of their value as cultivators. Jim had fixed up a shelter for them from sheets of corrugated iron, lined with straw, encased in wire-netting. This he had placed in an enclosure on a piece of rough ground, full of couch grass and heather. The whole thing, shelter and enclosure, was movable. Our idea was for them to bull-doze and fertilise, bit by bit, this piece of ground, which could then provide first-class grazing for sheep and cattle. The piglets soon got the idea and the morning after their arrival their little pink snouts were black with burrowing in the peaty soil. Whatever it was in the way of vitamins and minerals they got out of the heather roots and the ground, I don't know, but they certainly did thrive. There was no lolling about in a clean, concrete sty for them, they worked for their living and they liked it. The exercise in the confined space certainly didn't prevent them putting on good, healthy flesh.

Neighbours came from far and wide to cast an eye over them, prod them with sticks, scratch their backs and murmur 'porky, porky!' into their appreciative ears. A pig does love to be flattered, and the neighbours would say, as they lit their pipes and shook their heads slowly from side to side, 'grand pigs, grand pigs...' in a ruminative, almost wistful way. In the old days, when weaners were to be had for half a crown, every croft had its pig, tenderly reared in a small, dark sty: in November it would be stuck and salted. Mrs. Maclean had given me the recipe for the brine mixture and told me tales of the great feastings they had always had with their Christmas ham. However, these particular little pigs were to go to market, and go they did a couple of months later, when they fetched more than double their purchase price and we bought six more with the proceeds.

That month we had a real heat wave. Warm, dry weather is so much the exception to the rule here that we tend to welcome it with open arms, and to revel in it unthinkingly. The heat shimmers over the moor, the hills are shrouded in blue haze, the scent of the small flowers is honey-sweet and lulling. Helen scampers around, in the briefest of sun-suits, and in no time at all is burned gipsy brown. But a heat wave brings its problems.

We hadn't had much snow that winter, the springs were running low and to our dismay we found that there was not enough of a flow to drive the pump at the well. The storage tank in the house was empty and we began a frantic search for an additional supply. We wished the golden well were not so far away, it would have solved all our problems. Neighbours, sympathetic as always to our troubles, told us of several spots where they remembered water rising long ago. We followed their directions and eventually came on the old 'horse well', where our predecessors had always watered the horses. It looked promising. Jim and Billy cleared the rushes, dug down to the source of it and laid a pipe, to connect the flow with that from our existing source. It was not strong enough to make much difference immediately, but we were confident that it would help after a good spell of rain. In the meantime, we had to carry water for drinking and cooking in pails, every morning and evening, while for washing we still had some in the big butt at the back door. When that was done I carried the clothes down to the near burn and laundered them there. It was very pleasant on a burning hot day. I would lay the linen on a flat stone and rub it clean, then rinse it in the clear flow. Now and again, an astonished trout would flash through the washing pool: a frog would give me an incredulous stare before bounding to the safety of a cool, green hollow in the bank. When my back began to ache I would stretch out on the grass and watch Helen splashing in her own pool upstream.

Dinner would be a picnic eaten on the doorstep that day, and I would make up for it by producing ham omelette and a cool salad at supper-time. I am thankful that eggs agree with us all and that they can be made into an almost endless variety of dishes. An egg and a lettuce, bread, butter and milk—I think we could all live on those for ever!

One evening, after a blazing day, which had left us really limp, we noticed the sky clouding at sunset. Helen was asleep upstairs, the chickens and ducklings had all gone to roost. Everything was very still and quiet and we were sitting in the cool of the living-room, looking through the papers, when I felt my ears twitch. I listened intently: it was the sound we had been waiting weeks to hear—the patter of rain on the tin roof of the scullery. We jumped up and looked out. The branches of the rowans were stirring, a breeze was rising and the rain was hissing on the parched ground. I think no sailor on a waterless raft in mid-Pacific ever greeted a thunder-plump as deliriously as we did!

In a remarkably short time the water-butt was overflowing. As we couldn't bear to see this water going to waste, I struggled into gum-boots, mackintosh and sou'-wester and put every available pail, basin and bath, in turn, under the overflow spout. Jim quickly bored a hole in the scullery window-frame, inserted a length of rubber tubing in the top of the butt, passed it through the hole and into the sink. To see the sink filling with this lovely, soft rain-water sent me nearly crazy with delight. We rushed in and out carrying pails, till we were soaked to the skin, our eyes bright in our gleaming faces. The supply of water we accumulated that night lasted us until the weather resumed its normal dampness.

We had a really grand crop of potatoes that year, at the cost of a deal of labour and anxiety. The field they were in had borne such an exceptionally heavy growth of corn the year before that the weeds had been well smothered. It had been ploughed each way, in the spring, so that the tilth was as fine as one could wish. We had borrowed a ridge plough to open the drills. The planting had been heavy work, but with three and a half of us on the job we had managed it fairly quickly. Then came the closing of the drills, a tricky operation with a tractor. The implement being in one's rear, it is the easiest thing in the world to knock the tubers out of place when covering them, with the result that they are liable to come up unevenly spaced, or through the side of the drills, or even in the spaces between the drills. Many people prefer to use a horse-plough to close the drills as, by this method, you can see exactly where you are and have greater control of your implement. However, Jim was determined to use the tractor and, at bottom, we applauded his courage, but our hearts were in our mouths as we watched the great, shining blades scattering the nicely placed tubers in all directions.

After completing the first few drills, Jim got into the way of the work and the crop certainly seemed to be covered, Next day we went up and down the field with hoes, pushing an odd tuber here and there into place. Then other things claimed our attention and we had to leave the potatoes to their fate.

Soon we began to cast an anxious eye over the field. Sure enough, the dark green, crinkled shoots were coming through the ground in the most unexpected places. The field, which had hitherto had the beautiful symmetry of a chessboard, now began to look like something that had come out in a rash.

We refused to be dismayed. Each armed with a hoe, we worked up and down the field, pushing and scraping, until we had virtually transformed each drill into a space, and vice versa. The effect was slightly irregular, of course, but when the plants came to maturity the leafiness of them hid the waywardness of their ranks and they were a noble sight. The heavy hoeing had killed every would-be weed at birth and the potatoes had it all their own way throughout the summer.

The turnips, too, were good that year, though by the time we finished singling them we felt we'd been born with a hoe in our hands. Smack, pull, smack, pull we went, day after day, along the interminable drills. We saw turnip seedlings sprouting in our dreams and wished the cows were not so desperately fond of the things. It was only the thought of being able to dump a pailful of succulent slivers under the nose of a stalled beast on a winter morning that kept us going. A turnip is indeed a handy thing to have about the place in winter: it gives a savour to the family soup pot; the hens love to peck away at one, when the snugness of their deep-litter house begins to pall and they're longing for a little diversion; and the sheep will gladly polish off any still left in the field, in the hungry gap of early spring.

We managed to keep the garden fairly clear of marauders that summer, though every time I went up to get a lettuce or an apronful of peas, I dreaded what I might find in the way of damage done overnight. The black-faced sheep has all the instincts of a mountaineer and is quite able to scale, or barge through, an ordinary wire fence. Cows have elasticated necks, with an amazing reach, and a distinct fondness for flower-heads of all kinds. Anything growing on the other side of a fence has an irresistible attraction for them. I sometimes wonder what they secretly made of the taste of the luscious-looking nasturtium leaves they devoured. Then there were all the other garden enemies—the goat, rabbits and moles and hares. Even the chickens were most unhelpful; in the early part of the season, when they were on free range, they would fly over the fence and scratch up the new-sown seed in a kind of demented frenzy.

One morning, I found Charlie, the horse, standing with a rather shamefaced, bewildered look in his eyes, in the midst of the trampled cabbages. It transpired that the children had left the gate open the evening before, Charlie had wandered in, the gate had blown to and he couldn't get out again. It was surprising, really, the small amount of damage he had actually done. I think he'd had a conscience about it! Anyhow, he seemed glad enough to be released from his enforced captivity among the vegetables.

It was a minor miracle that even one carrot should survive in the face of all these hazards. Our appreciation of the perilous journey which each bit of greenstuff or root had endured, before it reached the dish, gave an added savour to our meals.

All in all, that was a good year for the garden. The currant bushes, which a neighbour had given us, began to bear fruit. Mint, parsley and chives were all flourishing, along with carrots, parsnips, radish, peas, beans, chicory, beetroot, spinach and all the usual greens. There were even a few knobbly cauliflowers. In his few spare moments, Jim had made a glass-house on a framework of scrap picked up at the Inverness yard. I had high hopes of producing tomatoes in this and I did put a dozen plants in home-made compost in margarine boxes. But they took too long to ripen, in the meagre heat, and only developed some rather tight, pale balls of fruit, which I made into chutney. However, I found the glass-house an excellent place for bringing on flower seedlings, and subsequently it was put to other uses. It served as a brooder-house for day-old chicks and it once saved the lives of some weakly piglets. One year it grew a vegetable marrow and it now produces strawberries and mushrooms and gives us some most welcome out-of-season lettuce. It has done much to add spice to our lives and it has become quite a landmark. Sun and moonlight glisten on its roof, making it wink cheerfully across the landscape.

In a small enclosure off the garden Jim had placed our much-travelled beehives and he liked to talk bees with anyone who was interested. Every croft had its hive or two, but there were no real enthusiasts in the district. However, word soon got round that Jim was bee-minded and he travelled miles to collect swarms. The real bee-man is born, not made, either you have a feeling for the little creatures, or you haven't. Jim undoubtedly has; he works away quite unconcerned among them, scorning hats, veils and other protective apparatus. There is only a short clover season here, but the heather is right on the bees' doorstep and they were soon revelling in it and laying up another small harvest for us.

Our cattle all passed another tuberculin test, but Hope suddenly became alarmingly ill. On entering the byre one morning for the milking, she lay down in her stall and refused to move. Her stomach was swollen like a balloon and she was groaning in a most distressing way. We thought she had probably overeaten herself in the lush summer grass, and was blown. If that were the case, the only remedy, we knew, was the drastic one of plunging a sharp instrument into her side, to release the accumulation of gases—and we knew it had to be done at once, if she was to be saved. We looked at one another, wondering who would have the courage to perform the operation. Then, by great good luck, we happened to notice the vet's car drawing up at Willie Maclean's; he was on his testing round. Billy was despatched with an urgent message and, within a quarter of an hour, the vet was examining Hope. She was not, he said, blown, the swelling, apparently, was in the wrong place for that. With a mighty, combined effort we got her to her feet and he gave her a drench and told us to keep her in the byre, with her forelegs higher than her rear. We obeyed instructions and she slowly recovered, but she had very little milk for some time after that.

We were thankful disaster had been averted. The loss of a cow, on a small place such as ours, can be a very serious matter indeed. The result of this mysterious affliction was that Hope failed to come into season at the appropriate time. It is most important on a bleak, hill farm to have the calves born about April or May, so that cow and calf get the benefit of the good weather. To this end, the cows must be served in early or mid-summer. With some beasts you can detect at once the restlessness which means that they are, in local parlance, 'wanting away'. Immediately, you sling on the rope halter and allow yourself to be dragged the up-hill mile to the bull's domain. If you're lucky, the one trip will suffice, if not, you may have to accompany the wayward lady twice, or even thrice, on her nuptial journey.

With other beasts it is sometimes extremely difficult to detect the signs: they may occur only at night, when the household is asleep. You're lucky, then, if a kindly farmer will allow your cow or heifer to run with his bull for a lengthy period, to ensure satisfaction.

That summer, Hope had not the slightest desire to gallivant. In the end, in desperation, we had to get the vet to give her an injection, which had the desired effect of making her head post-haste bull-wards. We have since spent many anxious hours trying to anticipate the moods of various members of our small herd and have often wished that artificial insemination were not such a skilled and costly business.

On the rare occasions when we had leisure to lean on a gate, in those early summer days, we couldn't help feeling a certain sense of achievement. The cattle and sheep were thriving, the pigs were rootling and putting on weight. The lambs were all safely inoculated and bid fair to become winners. The hens and ducks were still laying hard and the new pullets were making good progress. They were white Leghorn, crossed with light Sussex, and as trim and elegant as ballerinas. The potato and turnip crops were lush and green. There was a ripple through the young grass and the oats were showing a milky sheen. There was much to consolidate, much to improve, but we felt we had at least passed a couple of milestones on our road.

CHAPTER VIII
FIVE YEARS A-GROWING

On a hill croft, once the turnips are singled and the potatoes ridged, there is a lull until hay harvest. On the low ground, the hay is usually ready soon after the turnips are done, and the lull is between hay and corn harvests. With us, getting in the hay is generally a very anxious and long-drawn-out affair, which may well go on till it overlaps the cutting of the com, so that we're very glad of a respite before the grass is ready.

With most hill-people this respite takes the form of an expedition to the nearest moss to cut peat. A bus-man's holiday, if you like, for the work is hard. Still, days at the peats do have a feel of jollity about them. For one thing, they mean a change of scene, as some people have to go several miles to find suitable ground. Then it's work all can share and very often men, women and children from several crofts will join forces, the men to do the cutting, the women and children to stack the peats to dry. Food will be taken and a fire lit from old, dry heather roots, to boil the dinner kettle. There is always much leg-pulling and wise-cracking— communal work always goes with a swing.

Later in the year another expedition will be made, when the small heaps of peats will be built into larger ones. It is rather like making stocks into ricks. Then in the autumn the whole lot will be carted home and built into a stack near the house door. It's a harvest that hasn't much worry attached to it. Even if the weather is so bad that the peats never really dry out, they will still burn reasonably well. There is also a definite sense of satisfaction in making oneself independent of the coal-merchant. We should have liked to have cut peats that summer, but there was still a lot of pioneering work to be done in the way of fencing and draining and this had to have priority.

Peat-cutting apart, July is a less strenuous month than some and so it is the most suitable time to hold agricultural shows. The second Friday in July is the day of the traditional Wool Fair in Inverness. It is still called the Wool Fair, although no wool is sold at it now. Wool has its own Marketing Board these days and one has to abide by the rules and regulations in the selling of one's crop. But Wool Fair day still retains its atmosphere of holiday. It has become a horse show and sale and everyone who can possibly spare a day goes to the market place to see the sights, to meet friends and have a dram.

We had heard that it was still sometimes possible to pick up a Shetland pony for a fiver and we went in hopes of getting one for Helen. But evidently something had happened to either the supply or the demand or both, for the Shelties all reached nearer the twenty-pound mark that year. However, it was a delight to see the magnificent beasts that were put through the ring. A superb Clydesdale was withdrawn at close on a hundred pounds. One admired the spirit of his owner. He certainly looked worth an untold amount, with his arched neck, his burnished coat and his huge, powerful limbs. All working animals have a dignity about them that no beast kept for pleasure or sport ever achieves. They may have lost their wild, native pride, but at least they never fawn or whimper. They demand respect and they get it from the men who work with them and know their value.

The next day we had a visit from a dealer, who practically insisted on buying Charlie from us. We had the greatest difficulty in making him accept our firm refusal. Charlie was one of us, we said, even supposing he never did another day's work, as long as there was a bite for us there would be a bite for Charlie. Eventually we pacified the dealer with a cup of tea and saw him off the premises. He gave us a half-pitying look as he climbed into his magnificent car. From the corner of my eye, I could see Charlie kicking up his heels with joyful derision, in the lush pasture down by the burn, and I could have sworn he knew exactly what had been going on. From that day on, our attachment grew stronger than ever to our wise, old, tawny-coated Charles.

Finlay came one evening, with his cousin Tom and a lad from a neighbouring farm, to clip the sheep. Jim and Billy had made a fank of wooden palings, and we had the sheep safely penned before our helpers arrived. We went indoors, with satisfied grins on our faces, to snatch a quick cup of tea before the operation began. But we'd evidently underestimated the strength of mother-love. The ewes, separated from their lambs, which were bellowing pathetically round the outside of the fank, made one wild stampede, completely ignoring the admonitory snaps of young Bess, whom we had left on guard, and broke through the rails. Within seconds the whole flock was scattered and all our gathering was to do over again. Luckily, the squad arrived soon after this disaster. They had two experienced dogs with them and between us we soon had the situation under control. It's a fascinating thing to watch a good dog and a good sheep-man penning the last few obstinate members of a flock. Not a hint of force is used, but the eyes of man and dog never leave the bewildered beasts. From the side of his mouth the man now and then utters a brief command. With stick outstretched he points; then, with a sort of uncanny mesmerism, man and dog impose their united will on the sheep. They lurch into the fold, the gate clicks to. We relax and breathe more freely.

All evening the men worked away at the sheep with concentrated energy. There was only the sound of the clicking shears and of an occasional scuffle with an unruly beast. Now and then, Tom would crack a quiet joke and Billy would curse the midges. Helen and I went out to help carry the fleeces into the barn, then I put her to bed—and still the clipping went on. At last, at ten o'clock, it was done: the last sheep staggered to her feet and went lolloping off to join her offspring. A freshly shorn sheep is perhaps the most pitiful-looking object in the world. Bereft of its fine, shaggy coat, her outline is anything but imposing. Where, one wonders, is the fine, arrogant beast which stamped defiance when a dog came too near her lamb, only a month or two ago? Surely this ungainly body, swaying off on its spindly, bandy shanks, can't be hers? But it is; her lamb finds her as alluring as ever and is soon trotting happily at her side.

The men were glad of their ham and eggs that night and we all relaxed, bare brown elbows on the table, till the last tints of the sunset had faded from the sky.

Later, we packed the fleeces into the huge bags supplied by the wool-broker in Leith and carted them to the road-end, to await collection by the float. The first harvest of the year was secured.

Still the grass was not ready for cutting. I made up my mind, while there was time to spare, to tackle the re-decoration of the house, so I started with the bedrooms. They had been distempered, walls and ceilings, one in blue and one in pink, but the distemper was flaking. All I had to do, I thought, as I donned an old overall and tied my head up in a scarf, was to scrape this distemper off and apply a coat of cream wall-paint in its place. I took a scraper and began on the ceiling of the blue room. I soon found that the removal of the blue distemper revealed a layer of off-white beneath, and of some indeterminate shade of green beneath that. But, having made a start, I had to go on and I scraped till my arm and shoulder were almost burnt up with aching and my neck had developed a permanent crick. Helen, determined to take part in whatever was going on, scraped away laboriously at small sections of wall and practically removed the plaster right down to the hard stone!

I could only spend a limited amount of time at the work, for the cow and the hens and the garden, which were my particular provinces, had to be attended to and large meals cooked thrice daily. Gradually something began to emerge from the welter upstairs. A pleasant smell of fresh paint was wafted about the house and at last I was able to show some result for my labours. It was amazing, the impression of light and space and airiness the light cream paint-work gave to the bedrooms. When the floor-boards were restained and the grates painted black, we felt we had at any rate two really presentable rooms. That meant that the rest of the house had to be tackled, for the shabbiness of it was all the more apparent. I developed quite a passion for decorating and it was very satisfactory to see the transformation that could be achieved. I did the landing and staircase walls and worked my way down to the living-rooms. There I had to do some preliminary plastering-up and I felt quite a professional as I daubed away with plaster and trowel. We left the kitchen to the last, chose a fine day, carted everything movable out on to the grass and went at it together, for the kitchen can never be out of action for long. The effect of the light paint there was quite dazzling, for hitherto the wood-work had been a most depressing drab brown. Finally, I painted the front door and the window-frames a rich blue, which gave a welcoming gleam to the house.

While these absorbing operations had been going on in the house, the grass had been quietly and steadily ripening. One warm, still morning, Jim hitched the mower to the tractor and, with Billy perched precariously on the swaying seat, guiding the blades, moved slowly along the edge of the field. I couldn't be expected to concentrate on cooking stew and apple-pie that day, even in my dazzling kitchen. Every few minutes I would be poking my head outside to get a sniff of the new-cut grass. Helen was trotting round in the wake of the mower, gathering flowers and shouting encouragement to the men. There was a feeling of excitement about. Miraculously, for that first hay harvest of ours, the weather held. One calm, blue day followed another and there was just enough stir in the air to dry the crop satisfactorily. We borrowed Bill-the-post's horse-rake and Charlie plodded up and down gathering the grass into windrows. We turned it and made it into small ricks and hardly a drop of rain came to interrupt the work. Grass, cut at the right moment, quickly made and dried by sun and wind, has a high protein content, whereas the stuff that's been sodden and turned over and over again, and only dried at last into a stiff, dark tangle, has little feeding value and will only serve to fill a void in a beast's belly. In subsequent years we've wrestled with hay till, near the point of exhaustion, we've sworn we'd never bother to cut the crop again. We've hung it on the fences, like washing, to dry, we've seen the ricks collapse into a black, treacly mess, we've had every kind of hay disaster, but that first crop was really a pleasure to handle.

Jim decided not to make the precious hay into stacks, but to store it under cover along at the far steading. There was no proper loft, but he made ceilings in byre, stable and barn by stretching wire-netting from wall to wall below the rafters. Then he stuffed the hay into the spaces between ceiling and roof. Billy looked doubtfully on this operation. It was certainly an innovation, but it worked.

The hay kept perfectly through the winter, except in one portion where the snow blew through an ill-fitting skylight, and the insulation kept the building warm. For feeding purposes it couldn't have been handier. All one had to do was to take a fork and tumble the hay down on to the hungry beasts below.

The only interruption to our days of haymaking that summer came not from the weather but from the four porkers on the heath. They were by this time massive creatures, with strong wills of their own and highly developed bumps of curiosity. They would stand on their hind legs, snouts resting on the rail of their enclosure, scanning the alluring horizon. The combined pressure was usually too much for the fence, sturdy as it was. There would be a crack and a clatter, and a tally-ho from Helen, 'the pigs are out!' We would drop whatever implement we were holding and rush to head the four great hulks off from the cornfield. Sometimes they would be too quick for us and would go crashing into the corn, making four separate runways through the beautiful up-standing stalks. Now and again they would pause and turn to leer at us out of their mischievous, unblinking eyes. I believe they thoroughly enjoyed those chases and indulged in them for sheer devilment. We found them exasperating and exhausting, so much so that we decided the only thing to do was to pack the porkers off to market. They strongly resisted our combined efforts to load them on the float. The driver lost his temper, the lovely summer morning air was defiled with raucous shouts and we made several picturesque additions to our growing vocabulary of the vernacular! But at last we waved them off and at the end of the day they covered themselves with glory by fetching quite spectacular prices at the market. Jim was so elated that he bought six more youngsters at once. We worked late that night, preparing a clean place for them on the heather.

We also sold the goats and have not since then had any more truck with the capricious tribe, for we found them more bother than they were worth. Tethered, they are a constant worry. They have to be continually moved to fresh ground and one is tormented by the thought that that muffled groan one caught, when upstairs making the beds, was one of them strangling herself. One rushes down and out, only to find it is a ewe which has temporarily mislaid her lamb. On free range goats are horribly destructive. In theory of course they rid the place of thistles and other noxious weeds, but in practice, when they're not in the garden selecting the most succulent of the greens, they're having a nibble at the bark of a beloved tree. Trees are so scarce and so precious here and we only have the one thin line of rowans to remind us that trees really do exist. The goats gnawed the bark off several, thus slowly killing them. I found the goats far more difficult to milk than any newly calved heifer. It always took two of us to do the job—one to hold and the other to extract the milk, and at the end of this tedious business there would only be a couple of pints, at most, at the bottom of the pail. We had heard the story of the wonderful nanny, who lived on practically nothing, came into the scullery of her own accord, morning and evening, to yield ungrudgingly her quota of creamy fluid and was so devoted to the family that she couldn't bear to be left alone and even had to be taken out in the car for a Sunday run! No doubt this story was true, but the goat concerned must have been an exceptional lady. The idea of a goat is fascinating in the extreme, but the reality may be quite otherwise.

I think Helen was sorry to see ours go, but Jim and I couldn't bring ourselves to shed a tear. Helen was rapidly developing a personality. Rising five, she had become, as we imagined she would, remarkably independent and adaptable. Birth and death she accepted as she did sun, snow and the sprouting of the seed in her garden plot. Death, I think, sometimes caught her on the raw, particularly when it came unexpectedly, say, to an adored yellow ball of a chicken, but then another birth would come along and the shadow would be gone. She loved to bring Hope in for the milking and it was amusing to watch the tiny figure in blue dungarees, brandishing a hazel-wand and making the appropriate noises, while the great, brown hulk of the cow came swaying up the field and lurched into the open byre. She showed great concern for all the animals' welfare and would spend hours trying to restore a strayed lamb to its mother. She could hear and see with astonishing acuteness; it was a quiet world she lived in and any sound which came to disturb the quietness had to be interpreted at once. Bess had only to set up a barking, from her vantage point at the end of the steading, and Helen would come rushing in with the news. 'It's Feely (Finlay), Mummy, I see him coming along the heather with Tom. P'raps they want to borrow the mower.' It was more than likely that that was indeed the explanation for the hubbub. Once, it happened that I was the first to glimpse a loaded lorry coming down the hill road to the back of us. 'There's a load of straw for someone', I said, gazing at the vehicle, which looked like a child's toy, crawling down the slope. 'Not straw, Mummy, it's hay that's in it', Helen said, in a matter-of-fact tone. I looked again but, for the life of me, I couldn't have distinguished the greenish-yellow of hay from the golden-yellow of straw at that distance. To Helen, it came quite naturally.

She took an intense interest in the weather, understanding instinctively the effect it had on all our lives. The stars had a deep fascination for her. They are her bright lights. This fascination has grown, over the years, and her present ambition is to become an astronomer. Jim and I have exhausted our stock of knowledge of the subject and have imparted all the legends we know, too. We've given her two star-books and she often drags us out, on a glittering cold night, to identify planets and look for shooting stars. We wouldn't have it otherwise; we gladly suffer frozen toes and a crick in the neck so that she may revel in the blaze of the night sky. She is a great stickler for accuracy, and I'm certain that at the back of the statistics she's catching the steady gleam of poetry.

During that summer she began to get 'itchy feet'. She could already manage a hill walk of three or four miles, with us. Now she showed definite signs of wanting to go off occasionally on her own. Sometimes it would be to Woodend she'd go, sometimes over to the Macleans, where young Bertha was always ready for a game. We'd watch her progress from wherever we were working, see the small figure bouncing from tussock to tussock across the moor-ground, watch it disappear behind the raised bank at the burn-side and emerge seconds later on the other side of the water-splash. She was always sure of her welcome in the little house, where Mrs. Maclean would have a drink of milk for her, or lemonade, if the day was warm, and a pancake off the girdle and a sweetie for the way home.

She was big for her age, strong and independent, yet she was still not much more than a baby. Every day, after dinner and after supper, I used to take her on my knee and read her a story, from a book with large print and plenty of pictures. One day I suddenly realised that she was growing up. It was wet and I was mixing a cake in the kitchen. Helen was sitting quietly in the living-room. All at once she came to my side, dumped an open book in the midst of the floury mess on the table and began, quite calmly, to read to me. The words were simple and mostly of one syllable, but she hardly hesitated. I just held my breath and listened. It seemed like a minor miracle to me. To her, it was the simplest thing in the world, quite obviously. Since that day she has gone on reading steadily and our only difficulty now is to keep her supplied with books.

Helen found the wireless a great delight during that last pre-school year and she would caper round the kitchen to 'Music and Movement', tap with the poker to 'Time and Tune', and sing at the top of her voice with William Appleby. She even listened, enthralled, to the adventures with prehistoric monsters in 'How Things Began' and insisted on having 'Science and the Community' turned on full blast, though what she made of it none of us were sure!

She was never bored—every day brought something different to do. Times of celebration, such as Christmas, Hallowe'en and birthdays, were eagerly looked forward to and prepared for.

'How lonely she must be!' several of our friends said, at various times. They no doubt had a picture in their minds of one small girl surrounded by acres and acres of solitude and quiet. From the co-siness of suburbia, where there are iced lollies round the corner, shop-windows full of glittering toys, and a bus to take hordes of good children to the Saturday morning film show, this vision must have been something to turn from with a shudder.

Alone she undoubtedly is, in the sense that each one of us is alone, to the end of time. But she has learnt to face that aloneness from the start, she has grown up with it, so that she knows it's not a fearful thing. It will never become a bogy, to be dodged, but is already a companion she can walk with hand in hand. She has always had to do the last bit of the road from school on her own, along the track through the heather. Sometimes, if the day is really bad, we have hurried to meet her, for she still seems such a minute scrap of humanity, set against the vastnesses of hill and sky. But not once have we found her in the least disconcerted by snow, gale or thunder. She plods along, with a twinkle in her eye, taking whatever comes.

All in all, by the end of that second summer, we felt that our plan for Helen was working out better than we hoped.

CHAPTER IX
AN IMPROMPTU HOLIDAY

THE combination of hay-harvesting (comparatively easy though this had been) and house-painting, interspersed with pig-chasing left us, we had to admit, a little jaded, and the really big task of the year—the harvesting of the corn—was still to come. Everything was under control; the potatoes were in full bloom, the new pigs still at the amenable stage, the pullets settled in their deep-litter. Suddenly, simultaneously into our two minds, leapt the idea that a little holiday, just a long week-end, would be wonderful! We still had Billy. We might not have him another year, but for the moment we had him. We had never had the slightest qualm about leaving him in full charge when we had had to be away for a whole day at the market. He was as honest as daylight and well used to looking after himself.

Surely we could leave him to cope for the week-end? we asked ourselves. It was really more of a statement than a query and within twenty-four hours our minds were made up.

There is never any wondering with us what form a brief holiday shall take. We simply bundle ourselves, some bedding and some food into the old van and are off. That is half the joy of it, really, the knowledge that you can, within a matter of minutes, almost (though not quite!) as birds take wing, be on your way. There is no wearisome planning and contriving and agonising over expense. The van is there, we have to eat wherever we are, and a few gallons of petrol can't break the bank.

We decided to leave on the Friday and to be back by the following Tuesday afternoon. I unearthed the two inflatable rubber mattresses, an old cot mattress of Helen's and the warm sleeping-bags. I packed three biscuit tins with food, filled an egg-box, gathered an assortment of plates, cups, knives and forks, bathing suits, old rubber shoes, extra garments, the bivouac, a book or two and the camera, into a kit-bag, and we were ready for the road.

Where to go is never any problem; the west is in our blood and we simply gravitate towards it, as the birds migrate with the sun. Billy was most helpful and quite entered into the spirit of the thing. He even gave the van a clean-up and stuck a bit of canvas over a leaky portion of the roof, then he filled an extra can with petrol and stood by to give us rather a wondering farewell wave. Perhaps he doubted whether he'd ever see us all alive again.

It was drizzling, and certainly rather chilly, as we crawled up the 'overside'. We turned our heads at the top of the rise and glanced back at our little fields of ripening corn and potatoes and roots. The sheep and cattle looked small, defenceless dots in the distance. We felt a little guilty about leaving these well-loved tyrants of ours, even for a few days, but—'Ach, everything will be all right without us', we said, to ease our minds, and we chugged slowly north and west.

We went through Beauly, Muir of Ord and Garve—pleasant places all of them, but just a little tame. Then we swung on to the moor road and we knew we were really on our way. There was a grey mist over the hills and the burn was foaming amber after the rain. With every mile the authentic smell of the west came at us more strongly—there s nothing like it anywhere. It's made of the scent of wet heather and sea-tangle and mist and hill-air and it always goes straight to our heads. We opened the windows wider and poked our noses out, to get a delighted sniff. Helen clutched Duchess round the neck and began groping for her spade and pail.

We cruised along the side of Loch Broom into Ullapool, passed the last straggle of the village and looked for a turning to the sea. We knew we simply had to get our hands into sea-water that day. Another mile or so and we were bumping along a deep-rutted track towards a small lighthouse. Right at the point we came to a halt on a rise of bright green sward. Straight ahead lay the Summer Isles; the water between was gleaming in the pale, evening sunlight. We sat a moment looking and listening to the slapping of the small waves on the pebble beach. Then Helen, already shoeless, made straight down to the water's edge and we followed, strolling at leisure, as though there were all the time in the world for everything—the west had already imposed its rhythm on us.

From the contemporary point of view, the average west coaster is a failure: he has no ambition, no drive. Because he has no desire to be for ever 'bettering' himself, he is considered lazy and feckless. True, in former times many people from the west went to America and Canada, where some of their descendants have made names for themselves; we hear of the few, but of the many there is no record. It is not always realised that those emigrations were, in most cases, enforced by the ruthless, alien landlords, who emerged after the real clan system had broken down. The men were driven to the boats, the women and children were carried aboard, and the songs which drifted back across the water as the boats put out were laments, bitter, hopeless laments. Many a settler would sit, years afterwards, looking across the 'waste of seas' and in his dreams 'behold the Hebrides'. He had no natural desire to leave his native coast—why should he? Times might have been bad, but they might be bad anywhere. At least, as long as he was not interfered with, the west coaster need never have starved. Even if the crops failed utterly, he could get his fish from the sea and his bit of game from the hill. The seaweed itself made a tasty dish, full of iodine and health-giving minerals. And he had his horizon; he could see things in the light of infinity, which is the only way to get a true perspective. Why should he want to exchange all this, for a mad rush after money? What could money buy that wouldn't bring him envy and discontent, an aching head and ulcers in his stomach? The west coaster will leave it to others to achieve brilliance as politicians and administrators. He'll also leave it to others to become spivs or invent the nuclear bomb. Give him three rooms to house his family, a few acres and a boat and he's the happiest man on earth. He still believes in happiness.

These thoughts were in our minds, as we looked back across Loch Broom and saw the tiny fields sloping down to the water's edge. Every inch of ground was cultivated; the small patches of corn and potatoes and roots were bright and flourishing. The natural manuring of the beasts, plus the application of seaweed and shell sand, has resulted in a high degree of fertility in the crofting ground. The Cheviot sheep that were grazing right down to the water's edge looked remarkably fit and strong. Hay-making was in full swing and every available pair of hands was busy hanging the grass on tripods to dry.

When Helen had dabbled to her heart's content in the clear, green water, we looked for a spring, gathered driftwood and built a fireplace. Soon, ham and eggs and tomatoes were sizzling in the pan and we ate a leisurely meal, washed down with hot, delicious tea, and stretched ourselves on the turf in relaxation. Sun, moon and stars were to be our timepieces for the next few days. Our watch was not reliable, anyway, and we wanted to discard all sense of urgency. There was no cow to be milked, there were no pigs or hens to feed, no eggs to collect, no weeds to watch for—there was nothing to hinder our entry into timelessness. And that is surely as near as we'll ever get to a glimpse of the infinite, this side of Styx.

When Helen began to yawn I unrolled her mattress and placed it across the two front seats of the van. Jim collapsed the other seats, to make the back part flat, and we blew up the rubber mattresses and laid them lengthwise there. Duchess was accommodated in the bivouac, along with the stores.

Helen was asleep in a couple of minutes. Slowly, we washed and dried the dishes and made ourselves another brew of tea, while the sunset colours faded from the sky and little flashes of light began to wink out from the far headlands. We were loath to sleep. Why, at any rate in summer, did people bother to live in houses? we wondered, and we found again the contradictions in ourselves. We loved our own small house, every stick and stone of it. We loved the bonds that held us to the work of cultivation, and we knew every corner of each of our fields. To see them in good heart gave us the deepest kind of delight. To watch something edible, anything, even a lettuce, grow, where nothing but weeds had grown before, was the most satisfying thing we knew. Yet here we were, completely happy as nomads! We had unearthed an even deeper level of existence.

Jim tells me that the Stewarts have always been quite content among the tinkers and I, a Stewart by adoption, would be happy to join forces with them. After the '45 Rebellion, many of them were obliged, like others of the resistance movement of the time, to take to the hills, and their descendants to this day find it difficult to conform. Every summer some of them pitch their small, brown tents on the edge of our moor and make tin pans for us, in exchange for our discarded scraps of clothing and shoe-leather. Their brown faces are lean and wrinkled, but their eyes are bright, and we've heard them in the evenings scraping away at a fiddle for the fun of the thing, with no one in miles to throw them a sixpence. They're not exactly useful members of society, perhaps, but they keep their own particular brand of integrity while many a County Councillor has lost his, somewhere on the way. Who knows?— they may make a better death on a bundle of heather under the stars than he will on his sprung, quilted bed.

In the morning we were all awake early and we lay, snug in our sleeping-bags, watching the fishing fleet sail into Loch Broom. The sea was a dazzling glitter of blue and gold. The sky was a vast, crystal dome. It was a morning of ceremonial splendour. The normal climate of the west is damp and sunless, maybe, but, funnily enough, on nearly every occasion when we've been there, we've come on these splendid, colourful days.

After breakfast we went down to the beach and dabbled in the water. Helen had a dip and we looked for agates among the pebbles. It wouldn't have surprised us that morning if we'd discovered gold! We gathered more driftwood and watched the gulls gliding over the sea, and the day slipped away over our heads.

We got into our sleeping-bags quite early in the evening and lay watching the sunset, till we could almost identify ourselves with each shred of cloud about the sky, each gleam of light, each shaft of colour. All the petty aches and worries that ruffled the surface of our daily working lives were smoothed away, as we made contact with these remote, unearthly things. They were with us all the time at home, but there we viewed them differently. When we looked at the sky, it was usually to try to foresee what kind of weather was in store—rain to swell the root crops or sun to ripen the grain. Now, we could see the sky as sky, a law unto itself, not necessarily something which would further our own small ends. Moments of detachment and reassessment are vivifying. One such moment, if it is sufficiently intense, may leave an impression on the mind that will withstand a lifetime of living. The universe is not a cosy place specifically designed to suit human needs. If everyone could grasp that fact afresh every morning, perhaps we should spend less time thinking up ways to exterminate one another. We should be grateful, as the tinker is, for a blink of sun to warm our bones in summer and the friendliness of a rock cave to shelter us from snow; we should be in touch again.

Sunday we spent wandering along the cliff-top to the next bay. St. Martin's Isle lay green and deserted in the middle of it. Saints had a liking for islands and I can see the point. It's sometimes difficult to remain sufficiently an island unto oneself, but to live on one perpetually does seem rather like dodging the issue. The difficult thing is to stay in touch on the land mass. There are many more saints than those recorded in the annals of holiness.

Helen skipped ahead of us on the springy turf. She was a small, lithe slip of humanity, all right, yet she was part of the blue morning, the curving wave, the gliding sea-bird, the withdrawn sky. The sight of her made us feel clumsy and awkward, with our loads of living pressing on our shoulders.

We made for the beach and let the clear water swirl about our ankles. We found beautiful fluted, moulded shells, smooth coloured pebbles, swathes of glittering sea-weed. We gulped down lungfuls of ozone. The world was one vast morning, brimful of light, and we understood why the Gael has for his promised land 'TIR NAN OG', the land of youth.

As we came back within sight of our camp, in the late afternoon, three large, brown cows looked at us with startled eyes and went lurching off across the sward. What had they made of our intrusion into their domain? we wondered. A moment later we knew the answer—they had certainly made the best of it. The pan that I had left filled with scrubbed potatoes, ready for our evening meal, had been overturned and its contents had completely disappeared. A cow does love a tattie! And so do we, when we're ravenous, after a long day in the air. There was nothing for it but to fetch water and scrub another lot of potatoes for supper. Within the hour, we were sitting cross-legged round the fire, eating mashed potatoes and poached eggs and drinking gipsy tea. There was magic in the air, the pure and simple magic of being alive and in touch with the moment.

Next day we decided to make for Gruinard Bay and spend our last night there, before pushing home. I remembered it from some twenty years before, as an enchanted place, where the green water came foaming over dazzling white sand. It had been to me then a 'faery-land forlorn'. There was a wide sweep of turf, I remembered, where we could make our camp. We went round by Dundonnell and the shore of Little Loch Broom and we passed an alarming number of notices announcing 'Teas' and 'Bed and Breakfast', outside croft houses, which looked hardly big enough to accommodate their owners, let alone stray visitors. I took a look at the map, though there could be no question but that we were on the right road. Then the cars began, and the caravans, and the droves of cyclists. Twenty years before it had been an event to meet one crofter on the road, driving his cow or his sheep to pasture.

As we came round the last bend, into the sweep of the bay, we had to draw sharply into the side of the road, for a large sports car nearly had us ditched. The green sward was dotted with cars, caravans and tents of every description. In the one clear space some youths were kicking a football about. At the roadside stood a large receptacle, clearly labelled 'Refuse'. If it had served its purpose one could have forgiven it for being there, but the refuse was all too obviously littered here, there and everywhere, on the sand, the grass, the road.

When my dismay had subsided a little, I began to appreciate that it was an excellent thing that others had discovered this place. One should, of course, never hug a haven to oneself. I saw the fat, brown babies staggering about the caravans, the mothers lying with their toes in the sand. It was good that they should be there, but in my shared paradise I'd make a law that everyone must bury their rubbish, under penalty of expulsion.

It was getting late as we drew into the only secluded spot we could find, at the far end of the bay, beside a burn. Helen sped across the sand and into the water. She was in Abraham's bosom still, and saw only what she wanted to see. The water was as clear, the sand as soft as it had ever been.

We had supper early, for mist was coming in from the sea, and crept into our sleeping-bags. Then the midges began! We swatted and slapped at them then tried to smoke them out. We covered ourselves in lotion and buried ourselves completely under the covers. Nothing was any good; we lay scratching and tossing through the small hours. At last, at about five o'clock, we could stand it no longer so we dragged on our clothes, flung everything into the van and made off.

We crawled up the long, steep rise to the next headland, where a delicious breeze met us. We stopped and let it play round our hot, aching limbs. Only then, in the lovely early sunlight, did we really examine the damage we had suffered. Our faces, arms and legs were covered with lumps and blisters of a most fantastic size— it would have been funny if it hadn't been so infuriatingly irritating. We daubed ourselves with lotion again and as we were doing so, a shepherd passed by with his dogs at heel. 'Aye, it's a fine morning', he said, and he couldn't quite manage to hide the astonishment in his eyes as he saw us doctoring ourselves at the roadside so early in the morning. He would never have dreamt of commenting on it, of course, and after we'd agreed about the fineness of the weather we had a talk with him about the progress of his lambs and other shepherding matters. We could picture his wife enjoying the little tit-bit of news he would relate to her that evening over his supper!

We made a fire, boiled our kettle and cooked our bacon in the lovely breeze on the headland. Our spirits rose, as our blisters subsided, and we began to look about us with calm eyes again. By mid-morning we were at Gairloch and we had to stop for half an hour there to let Helen have a last scamper on the sand. Then we took the road along the side of Loch Maree to Kinlochewe, thence to Garve and our own territory. All the way, with our backs to the west, we were wishing we could turn about at the next bend. But that's the way a holiday should end; we'd caught it on the wing and we knew it would be with us for good.

Billy met us with his usual, cheerful grin, and we saw at once that all was well. We went the round of the animals and cast a loving eye over the fields. Then, as it was wet, we made a fire in the hearth and sat quietly at it, content to be hugged by our own four walls again.

CHAPTER X
'GRAND LAMBS!'

AFTER that holiday jaunt of ours we found we had, from time to time, to indulge our urge to wander. We spent several long afternoons gathering brambles at Loch Ness-side. I think they must be the most succulent brambles in the world, those that grow with their roots in the water. The loch-side is the ideal place for a gipsy meal: there's driftwood for a fire and natural shelter in the tangled undergrowth should it rain. An expedition down there never fails to yield treasure. In spring, there are primroses, willow catkins and violets; in summer, bluebells and wild strawberries; in winter, holly berries. Autumn, of course, is the most fruitful season. There are sloes with a bloom on them like that on hot-house grapes, and brilliant haws and rowan-berries. Under the trees grow many kinds of fungoids, including the bright red, white-spotted, fairy-tale variety. I often wish I could be sure which were the edible ones, so that we could put them in our stew, as the French do. The brambles we make into jelly and jam and also, by simply steeping them in sugar, into wine, which looks, and even tastes, very like port. The rowan-berries from our own trees we always make into wine. I have sometimes made jelly from them, but even with the addition of apple it's rather bitter as a tea-time spread, and really only popular as a relish with meat. The wine is child's play to make. You simply pour boiling water over the berries, add a small piece of root ginger and let them steep for ten days. Then—bottle! After a year or so maturing, this wine is really good, pale amber in colour and with quite a kick in it. A friend of ours was once given a glass of it and asked to identify his drink. He took a sip, rolled it round his mouth, smacked his lips and solemnly pronounced: 'Liqueur whisky!' For a moment, I thought he was pulling my leg. When I saw that he wasn't I felt quite gratified! I thought of the skirmishings that went on in these hills years ago over the distilling of whisky. I remembered the subterfuges and the heartbreak that the illicit business involved, the kegs which had to be thrown into the loch when the excisemen appeared on the horizon, the searchings that went on for years, though the precious stuff was never recovered. Yet here was I, openly making my brew, with no kind of apparatus at all, gaily bypassing all kinds of tariffs and restrictions and offering a sup to all and sundry. There is something to be said for living on one's hump. It would be a pity if the easy world-wide exchange of produce, which lines many a middle-man's pockets, should make us completely overlook the resources that are to hand. In the press-button age, when a minimum of effort for a maximum return is the slogan for living, what will be the spur to enterprise? The creative efforts of the few will leave the many gaping, incapable of wonder, blank-eyed with boredom. In these conditions, war might well appear a relief to the unending tedium. The thwarted child will revel in destruction; it's a means of drawing attention to his plight, if nothing else. Give a boy a mountain to climb and he'll forget all about wanting to kick his neighbour on the shins. He'll be only too thankful the other fellow is there, hanging on to the other end of the rope to steady him.

In our own life we had to plan for a scrap of leisure. We found it was comparatively simple, if no emergency cropped up, to organise Sunday into a day of relaxation. The animals would be fed a little later than usual, and by eleven o'clock all the necessary work would be done. Then six hours would lie before us, to be used as we liked. If we had had a heavy week at field-work, we were sometimes more or less obliged to divide this spell into two watches, during which one of us would stretch out upstairs, with a book, while the other indulged in some quiet ploy with Helen. Then we would relieve each other with a cup of tea at half-time. But most often, at any rate in summer and autumn, we would put an apple and a scone in our pockets and make off into the hills.

The more closely we lived with the hills the more compelling we found them. Away from them, we were never quite happy and a day in town had no real charm for us. Once our immediate business was done we would wander round, look into shop-windows, buy a weekly paper, have a cup of coffee, think to ourselves, 'This is a change, a relaxation, I'm enjoying this'. But we knew quite well we weren't, really. The moment of delight would come when we reached the top of the road again and saw the outline of the hills and smelt the tang of the high air.

On these Sunday expeditions we would get right into the folds of the hills. One of our best-loved places was the shore of a small, nameless lochan, half-way to Glen Urquhart. We would sit there on a calm day listening to the stillness. Helen loved this game. She would crouch, 'frozen', like a young hare, her eyes round, ears on the stretch, waiting to catch sights and sounds. We would watch a puff of wind rippling through the rushes and across the face of the water. A strange shape would come flapping across the sky towards us. 'A heron!' one of us would whisper and we'd watch the gaunt, grey form wing slowly closer and settle at last on the far edge of the lochan. We would lose it among the sedge, then find it again, and watch it laboriously probing the mud.

We would examine the mosses at our feet, peer into the heart of the tiny flowerets they sported, watch, fascinated, the scurrying of insects through the grasses. Most of these forms of life we couldn't put a name to: we knew nothing, really, of their ways, but the thing to do was to stay absolutely still and let them speak for themselves.

On the way back Helen would scamper ahead, leaping from tussock to tussock and as we neared our home ground we'd sing and tell each other stories and earnestly discuss what we'd most like for supper.

September is always an anxious month in these heights. Even though the hay is safely out of the way, as it usually is by then, there is always the fear that the corn will not be ready for cutting before the evenings close in. By that time the potatoes are ripe and the two harvests overlap; then there is one hectic scramble to get everything done in the short days, before the snow comes. That September the weather was extremely mixed. We would have all plans ready to make a start at the corn, when the wind would suddenly veer to the west and down would come the small rain. There would be nothing for it then but to stump off to the barn to do some tidying-up, or repair tools and implements. There is a quiet satisfaction in doing these jobs on a winter afternoon when there's nothing much else that needs doing, anyway. But to have to do them with your mind elsewhere and half an eye on the weather, knowing that the passing of each day is going to make the main business of the year trickier than ever, is frustrating in the extreme. As you sit in the barn, making stack-rope into coils, the beating of the rain on the iron roof sounds unnecessarily loud and even mocking.

That particular September we had every variety of unwelcome weather—rain, hail, thunder, the whole bag of tricks. At last, in the third week of the month, Jim made a start at cutting roads for the binder. Then we had to wait our turn for the 'binder-man'. At that time the Government tractor-service, a war-time innovation, was still operating. All the small places, which couldn't afford to carry a complete set of implements, were utterly dependent on it. It has since been abandoned and is sorely missed. Private contractors have taken over the work, but they charge much higher rates and are not so reliable. Many of them use inferior implements, which are liable to break down and hold the work up at crucial moments. We had, or could borrow, enough implements to cope with most operations ourselves, but for cutting the corn and threshing it we relied on the Government service.

It was the first of October before the binder at last came clanking its way into the cornfield, and that was the day the lambs were to be sold. Alec had helped Jim to pen them in the fank at the roadside. Finlay passed by on his way to the market and he cast an appreciative eye over the lambs and thrust knowing fingers into the wool on their well-padded flanks. 'Grand lambs', he said 'they'll top the sale, I'm thinking!' We smiled with pleasure. They were certainly good lambs, but as for topping the sale, well, there was surely a touch of poetic licence about that pronouncement! Yet hill-men don't usually exaggerate or risk judgement unless they are pretty sure of their ground, I reflected. However, I had no time to ponder the matter. I waved the float good-bye and immediately set to work, stooking in the wake of the binder. Helen helped too, and we staggered up and down with armfuls of sheaves, till it was time to boil die tatties for the binder-man's dinner.

By mid-afternoon we had a good row of stooks standing. Jim would be pleased that we'd managed not to let the sheaves accumulate, I thought. The rain began to come down in sheets, but still we kept on stooking, till I saw the old brown van nosing its way down the side-road towards us. Then, dripping wet, but happy, we made across the field to greet Jim. He thrust a grinning face through the open window. 'Finlay was right. The lambs did top the sale. Ninety-one shillings a-piece!' He stepped out into the rain and we gazed at each other, still hardly believing in our luck.

Then we all made for the shelter of the kitchen and celebrated with hot tea and scones at the fire. In those days, ninety-one shillings was a sale record. It is still a substantial price for a lamb straight from its hill grazing, not stuffed with fodder in a lowland park. We received congratulations from far and wide. On our next trip to town, Jim bought me a Stewart tartan jacket as a memento of the occasion. While the extravagant fit was on, I bought two rose bushes, one for each side of the front door.

Most of October the weather was even worse than it had been in September, but about the middle of the month we managed to snatch two or three days to make stacks. The three youngsters from across the burn came to help and we split into two teams, one with the tractor and trailer, the other with Charlie and the cart, and in this way we managed to rush the corn into the stack. We put in an order at once for the threshing-mill, for we were not sure about the keeping quality of the grain.

Meanwhile, the potatoes were ready for lifting, but the ground was far too soft to bear the weight of a tractor for the job. We dug several drills with graips. It was a back-breaking process, and we could see nothing for it but to leave half the crop in the ground till the spring. It has been done sometimes, with surprisingly little damage to the crop. At the beginning of November we borrowed a digger from some friends on the low-ground, whose crop was snugly pitted. We set to work hopefully with the tractor, but after half an hour or so the whole outfit got bogged. We tramped up and down, caked with mud from head to foot, groping for potatoes in the sodden ground. What fun potato-lifting can be on a sunny autumn afternoon, when the tubers come bobbing to the surface, as if by magic, in the wake of the spinner, and you scramble for them like children scrambling for a flung handful of pennies, and have time to sit on your up-turned pail for a moment's rest before the tractor comes round again! But that floundering in the quagmire was sheer misery.

Then everything took a turn. One morning, in the middle of November, when there was a hint of an Indian summer in the pale sunshine and the light, drying wind, we saw a little cavalcade approaching from the east. There was a white horse drawing a cart piled high with gear, a man and three boys. It was Alec with all the male members of his household come to lift our tatties with the horse and plough. It was the unexpectedness of this neighbourly gesture that really lifted our hearts. With a nod of greeting, Alec made straight for the field and hitched the plough to the horse. There are certainly times when the horse comes into his own, and this was one of them. It was heavy going, but by dusk we had a good few bags filled and carted to the pit.

Next day Alec came back with his boys and in the afternoon the threshing-mill arrived with a squad of eighteen helpers. Sadie came over to help me and never have I been so glad to greet her. It is always difficult to cater for a threshing squad. The day of their arrival is uncertain and hardly ever coincides with the visit of the grocer's van. You lay in a stock of butcher meat and do a huge baking for the day you expect them. They are sure to be held up at another place, and with the best will in the world your small family cannot eat its way through the joint and the mounds of scone and cake, and half of it has to go to the dogs. Then, on the day the mill does arrive, you have only tinned stuff and stale baking to fall back on, and your shame is great! However, this day, with Sadie's help, we managed to produce a compromise of a meal and the men were so hungry that they praised it quite wholeheartedly.

There is always a thrill of excitement about a threshing. The huge, unwieldy, yellow-painted mill has all the glamour and mystery of a piece of circus equipment. The steady humming of the mechanism suggests power without end, and the way the grain pours out in separate streams, one for each quality, seems like sheer magic to the uninitiated. The men tend the monster with steady, rhythmic movements of the arms, their faces set in serious lines of concentration. You can tell at once that machine-minding does not come naturally to them and there is a hint of the schoolboy's awe in their expressions. But when the tea-kettle and the baskets of scones appear and the noise of the mill subsides for a few minutes, they relax and gladly crack a joke in the returning calm.

Alec gave us still another day of generous help, while the weather held. Then the rain closed in again and we had to leave the last quarter of the field to chance. December came and frost and snow. We lifted several cart-loads of turnips and dumped them in an improvised shed. The fields were still wonderfully green, that is the one advantage of the late hill-season. The hungry gap comes all right at the end of the winter, when it seems as though spring is going to miss us altogether: but the back-end of the year can produce quite a tasty bite. However, once turnips are on the menu, the cattle go crazy for them. Life becomes one long round of carting, chopping and feeding turnips. Every beast about the place was partial to them, even the pigs, and fortunately we had a grand crop of them that year. They were so heavy that it was as much as I could do to carry two, swinging by their green tops, in each hand, from the field to the hen-house.

Our second lot of porkers were slower to fatten than the first had been, and they were developing rather unevenly. We put them under cover, along at the far steading, and stuffed them with potato stew. When we judged one of them was at last ready for market, we loaded him, after a terrifying tussle, into the back of the van, as it was not worth going to the expense of hiring a float for one pig. That was an epic journey, as Jim recounted it to me later. He had as front-seat companion a town friend, Mr. S., who was on his way to catch a train at Inverness. He was glad of the lift, but a little doubtful of his rear travelling companion. He himself was in his best rig, and spruced up for the occasion, whereas the pig was, to say the least of it, decidedly odoriferous! However, as long as they made up their minds to ignore each other, Jim thought he could manage to get them each to their destination. But a pig is an inquisitive creature. They had barely reached the main road when this one of ours, at a sudden jolt, broke loose from his moorings and thrust a grimy, inquiring snout against the back of Mr. S.'s shining collar. The unfortunate human passenger had, on Jim's instructions, to spend the rest of the trip scratching a bristly back with his soft, white fingers and murmuring 'porky, porky!' into a grubby ear, much to the delight of the pig and of the crowd of small boys, who peered incredulously into the van when it was held up at the first set of traffic lights.

That autumn we decided to avail ourselves of the services of a Government-owned ram, instead of buying one of our own. 'The Board', as the Department of Agriculture for Scotland is still called in these parts, undertakes to supply the crofter with one or more rams, according to his need, during the tupping season from November to January. One crofter in the district sends in a note of local requirements and arranges the distribution and subsequent collection of the rams. They are magnificent beasts and ensure a crop of high-quality lambs. The crofter pays four pounds for his ram, of which one pound is refunded if the animal returns intact from his tour of duty.

Only comparatively few crofts here have sufficient grazing to carry a flock of breeding ewes, but practically everyone takes in sheep from other parts for wintering. Some undertake to supply them with turnips, and make a higher charge for their boarders, others simply provide grazing on the outrun and the wintry in-bye fields. Others again find it profitable to buy in a score or so of Cheviot lambs once the harvest is secured, feed them on turnips and a little crushed oats and sell them before ploughing-time. As well as bringing in a cash return, the wintered sheep contribute to the well-being of the croft, by treading and manuring the ground. With their predatory habits they are a worry where fencing is anything but reliable, and are the cause of a good deal of heart-burning between neighbours, but their coming is part of the scheme of things and has to be tholed.

With the arrival of the tups and the winterings, we know that winter is really closing down on us. We've seen the great gaggles of wild geese come honking out of the cold north sky and watched them disappear into the evening haze, round the shoulder of the hill, and we've felt a little comforted to think that to these hardy creatures our bleakness is a refuge, that there are winter regions infinitely more desolate than ours. We've seen the fieldfares strip the last of the berries from the bare branches of the rowans and we're glad now of the cheerful company of the chaffinch flocks about the barn door.

There is, in spite of everything, a sort of cosiness about winter, a drawing-together of man and beast, in shared mistrust of the elements. The byre is an inviting place at dusk on a cold December day. It is filled with the sweet scent of dry grass and clover and of the breath of healthy cattle-beasts. The cows rattle their chains and turn their heads inquiringly, as we stagger in with armfuls of straw and hay and pailfuls of turnips. The hens 'sing', as they scratch contentedly away at the dry litter in their brightly lit quarters. Charlie comes to the doorstep, morning and evening, and stands rattling the door-knob till we give him his 'white drink', a pailful of water, with the chill off it, and a handful of oatmeal scattered in.

It's in winter that we realise fully how interdependent we all are. Also we have the satisfaction of seeing the result of our summer work in the fields. Perhaps only on a very small farm such as ours, where practically everything is produced for immediate home consumption, can these results be so startlingly apparent. We can almost identify each turnip we place in the slicer. As we throw a log on the fire, we sometimes pause to gaze at the flames licking it and murmur: 'That's a bit of the dead birch we had such a job to get over the fence.'

Life on a large farm can be almost as much a matter of mechanics as life in a factory or office. On a croft there is the intimacy and warmth of immediate contact with the fundamentals, and there is wholeness. What chance has the factory worker, who stands all day at his bench making an infinitesimal part of some giant machine, or the city typist who taps out another's words in triplicate, of acquiring wisdom or judgement, the capacity to see things in the round. Even the leisure of these unfortunate people is drained away in evenings spent gaping at the cinema or television screen. The penny-in-the-slot machine churns out the daily requirements of living. It can be quite pleasant to jog along with the blinkers on: those who still like to see the beginnings and the ends of things are considered uncomfortable finnicks.

To wrestle with things in the raw is a craving of every healthy human being. The height of happiness to a child is to scramble up a tree, to plowter through mud, to find shelter in a rock. The more scratched and torn and filthy he gets in the process, the wider his grin of delight when he staggers home. Deprived of this natural outlet, a city boy will find satisfaction in breaking windows, in slashing cinema seats or other boys' noses. If the immediate matter of making his living were one where a man could use the whole of himself—his strength, his wits and his imagination, the problem of how to fill his leisure would not arise, and he would be too preoccupied to spend more than the odd day thinking up ways to exterminate his fellows. His culture would not be imported in canisters from the other side of the world; he would make it himself, from a brain and a heart kept bright and taut with satisfactory living. It may be fascinating to have a picture of life among the peasants of Andalusia flashed to one's fireside, but how much more fascinating it would be to feel a song of one's own dancing on one's own lips out of the joy of one's own doings.

A natural life has its own tensions, its own moments of fulfilment and disaster, out of which art can leap unfettered, as a man tries passionately to record his glimpse of the pattern. For those who are not artists, there is the satisfaction of craft. I've seen it in the face of the man who selects a hazel branch from the thicket by the loch-side and slowly fashions it into a crook. In his strong, stubby fingers, the living wood is shaped and smoothed into an object that's not only vitally necessary to his daily work, but is beautiful into the bargain. He has made dozens of these crooks, yet no two are alike, each has its own individual feel in the hand.

Of course we can't put the clock back. We've got to go on from noon. At noon our inventions lie about us, glittering in the light like new-made toys. Where will we get the wisdom to lay hands on the wonders and to discard the monstrosities among them?

CHAPTER XI
THE BIG GALE

ABOUT the middle of December occurred one of those minor miracles, which are apt to be left out of a normally well-reasoned forecast of events, and which we have learnt to accept as tokens of beneficence. After a spell of snow, which had blocked the road and held up the grocer's van again, we suddenly emerged one morning into a day of blue and gold, with sunshine enough to set the midges dancing. We could hardly believe in it, yet we had to admit the evidence of our senses.

Our one thought was—the potatoes! As soon as the routine jobs were done, we made a final assault on the potato field. The frost had hardened the ground sufficiently to allow the digger to get a bite, and yet had not been severe enough to damage the tubers. In two days stolen from spring, we got the remaining drills lifted, and so our epic struggle with the potato crop ended in victory.

We needed every tattie we could lay hands on, for the pigs were consuming them in ever increasing quantities, and we sold none that year. Jim's ambition was to invest in a couple of in-pig gilts, in the spring, after all the porkers were sold. He had pig-fever badly. Small fortunes were being made in the pig-trade and we needed cash to build up the overall soundness of the place. Though it was a fickle business, liable to ups and downs unheard-of in the steady sheep and beef-cattle trade, we hoped we could catch it at an opportune moment.

Meanwhile, we lost Billy but we knew this was bound to happen sooner or later. He went to take up what had always been his main interest—the tending of sheep. We missed seeing him about the place. There was an elemental quality in him, a simplicity, a generosity, that was quite disarming.

'Little' Billy, from over the burn, who was gleefully approaching the end of his schooldays, began to spend every minute he could spare from home chores giving us a hand. He would work away all Saturday afternoon at whatever job Jim was busy at. After supper, he would play reel tunes on his mouth organ, while Helen cavorted about the kitchen. Those were happy evenings.

We passed the shortest day, confident in the knowledge that we were adequately prepared for winter. The whole of the year's effort is really directed towards this end. If the work has gone well, it results in a real snugness, with everything battened down and stores of food, fodder and fuel lying to hand, so that winter can be not only endured but positively enjoyed. If things have gone badly—a crop has failed or not been properly secured—then winter is a time of nagging anxiety, and sometimes the margin between the two states can be very narrow indeed.

By living thus, near to the bones of things, the simplest bounty can be a delight. It never fails to astonish me that the hens can lay eggs by the huge, golden dozen, while the snow is lying feet deep round their house and the wind is driving it through the minute crevices below the roof. True, we have worked all season to achieve this end: we've hatched eggs, or bought chicks at the appropriate time, we've spent hours liming and turning the litter of peat-moss, chaff and straw that warms the hens' feet, we've grown corn and potatoes to feed them, we've given them a light to simulate spring. Yet still it remains a marvel that the eggs are produced so ungrudgingly in the dark, bitter days. Similarly with the cow, the wonder is that the pail still brims with milk, though clover is only a memory wafted from an armful of hay.

The least co-operative of the animals were the pigs. Their job was to put on weight, and that is a thing no beast can be expected to do in a hurry, on a hill-top farm, in winter. However, we eventually shipped them, one by one, to market and though they didn't do as spectacularly well as their predecessors, they fetched quite satisfactory prices.

Christmas, as always, we made into a small oasis of light and relaxation. It's surprising that, in a part of the world as near the midnight sun as northern Scotland, there is no midwinter celebration like that held in Sweden, called the 'Festival of Light', when the youngest girl in the family, wearing a crown of candles, carries a light into every room in the house, shedding a beam into the darkest corners. Light is precious; it's fitting that there should be ceremonial in honour of the basic things. In the Catholic west, they still set a candle in the window on Christmas Eve to show the Child the way, but in the Calvinist north and east, Christmas passes almost unsaluted. However, I think our recognition of the Festival touched off a spring in the young people of the district. We returned home from a shopping expedition late one evening, hurried in at the front door and hastily changed into gum-boots and old coats before struggling out with torches to do the feeding round. I opened the back door and into my arms fell a mysterious object, dark, prickly and aromatic. A beam from the kitchen light struck it and I saw that it was shining with frost crystals. It was a Christmas tree, decked by nature! Tied to its trunk with a wisp of straw was a scrap of paper scrawled over with five words: 'Here is a tree. Billy'. It was the sheer unexpectedness of the gift that made the moment! We felt a glow in us, in spite of the numbness of our fingers, as we tossed hay and corn to the stalled beasts that evening.

Helen helped to decorate the tree that year. We dug up the tin of rowan-berries we had buried in the ground in autumn, and found they were as fresh and shining as the day they were picked. We collected fir branches and trails of ivy from the wood; and we had roast duck and apple sauce for our Christmas dinner. Then we gathered all the children about us and played games of magic by the fire.

Winter doesn't seem long when you have Christmas to prepare for and enjoy and New Year following close on its heels, with ceilidhs that go on till well into January. By the twelfth of the new month—date of the 'old' New Year, which is still kept in mind by the older generation here—there is 'an hour on the day', they say. It's a precious hour, for it means that you can do just that little extra bit of work outside before coming in for the night. You can repair a fence, or make a gate, or go after a strayed ewe, and indulge in a grin of satisfaction as you knock the snow from your boots and move the kettle on to the hot part of the stove.

'Whatever do you do with your evenings up there?' friends have asked us on several occasions, with an almost perceptible shudder in their voices. We sometimes wonder what we did with our evenings when we lived a town life; we just can't remember. Here, every one of them is memorable. To begin with, it is a joy to have achieved evening. We've been, say, sawing logs all afternoon, till the light has faded from mauve to green behind the hills. We've crunched our way about the yard feeding the animals, and we've come in with the pail of milk, the basket of eggs, the sack of fuel. We're pleasantly tired, and glad of shelter, and we've had a good hot meal, and tucked Helen into bed. Now there are books to hand, there may be some music we want to hear on the wireless, or a play. There is the diary to write, and a letter or two, and there are things to mend, events to be discussed, plans to be made.

Sometimes the door will open and in will come a neighbour without knocking. The absence of a knock is a sign that we're accepted as friends, and it always delights us. The evenings are never long enough: our pet vice is to sit gazing into the fire hours after we should be in bed. Are we hopelessly unambitious, anti-social even? Is there something lacking in us that we are content with the company of one another, a few neighbours, the beasts which depend on us and the slowly swinging stars? I don't know. But I do know that it is very satisfactory to be content to find the family unit, the neighbourly unit, the man-and-beast unit fitting securely into the pattern of hill and field and sky. Dr. Johnson himself, who surely ranks among the sophisticates, once said: 'To be happy at home *is* the ultimate result of all ambition.'

With the turning of the year, we began to prepare for the big event in Helen's life—school. She was five years old and could already read and write and do simple sums. She had a naturally inquiring mind and was as eager to learn as a collie pup to chase sheep. The Abriachan school was quite accessible, only about a mile down the road from our gate. But at that time it had only six pupils, all but one of whom were boys. There was not much prospect of happy companionship for her there. To send her to the girls' school in Inverness as a weekly boarder was financially impossible. Besides, we both have strong feelings about boarding schools; they seem to create their own rather artificial, even unhealthy, climate. Youngsters reared in them often find difficulty later on in adjusting themselves to the extremes of temperature in the world outside. We would rather that ours grew hardy and resistant from the start, with a background of family and farm life to keep her on an even keel.

The children from the Maclean household had all been to Glen Convinth school, which was about two miles away, on the Beauly road. One day, towards the end of January, we decided to walk over to see the headmaster of this school. Helen came with us, and we took exactly the road she would have to take—the path through the heather and across the burn to the Macleans' house, the short cut up the grassy slope and over the stile to the road, along the rise to the eleven-hundred-feet level and down the steep plunge to the wooded strath at the foot of Glen Convinth.

It was a brilliant day. The smoke from the few croft houses was rising straight into the still air. The Strathfarrar hills lay in a soft, blue haze. We reached the little grey-stone school, with its two high-windowed schoolrooms, and the Dominie's house adjoining. We noticed his neat garden, the apple-trees and the row of bee-hives. It was a pleasant place. I remembered the forbidding corridors and bare, windswept playgrounds of town schools and was glad Helen was to be spared those. Here there were two classrooms with a small lobby between. The huge branches of an oak were tapping the window panes. There was a grass patch edged with flowers for the children to run on. Behind the school building was a small, modern cook-house, where the midday meal was prepared.

We stood together, in the lobby, listening to the murmur of voices from the two rooms. Then we tapped on the door of the infants' room and a small lady, with a mother's face, came out to greet us. We told her we should like Helen to come to her school. She smiled, and went to fetch her husband from the senior room. He was tall, and looked a scholar. He wore a suit of rough Harris tweed, and when he opened his mouth out came the music of the western speech. We could feel at once the kindliness and warmth and humour of the isle-folk, and we knew Helen could not be in better hands than these. Having heard so much from town friends about the difficulty of getting a child into a school, we asked him somewhat diffidently if it would be all right to send Helen to him. Perhaps we were breaking some regulation, should she have gone to Abriachan school, which was nearer? He simply asked Helen her name, shook her hand and said: 'You come to school tomorrow, Helen.' And that was that.

We walked home in a happy mood. Through the half-open door of the infants' room we had glimpsed a row of small girls with fresh faces and old-fashioned ringlets. We thought of the fun Helen would have, the new games, the small, whispered confidences. We called in at the Macleans on our way home; they were delighted to hear that Helen was to go to Glen Convinth, and made plans for Bertha to meet her every morning at the burn and shepherd her to school. In the evening she was to wait for the bus which brought the scholars from the Junior Secondary school at Tomnacross to within half a mile of the stile and Bertha would see her safely to the burn again. In her ever kindly way Mrs. Maclean made everything seem simple and serene, and we felt confident as we sipped our tea at her fireside.

Two days later Bertha came over with a book from the school library for Helen. It was a kindly gesture on the Dominie's part and it gave Helen a taste for reading which has developed at an alarming rate over the years. We decided that she should start school as soon as the days began to stretch and the weather to soften a little.

January had been promising: we had had days when we'd been tempted to make a start at the ploughing. The bright air made it seem as though one small leap would land us in April—but we should have known better. On the last day of the month we were wakened early by the sound of a fierce north wind roaring up under the slates. We felt the whole house shake and give, like a ship in an Atlantic gale. We went down and peered out of the living-room window. Snow was being driven horizontally across the fields by a wind which must have been near to hurricane force.

Jim managed to open the back door and it took the two of us to shut it after him. He staggered out to see to the animals in the steading. I tried to light the fire in the kitchen stove, but I found that the force of the wind was so great that there was no suction in the chimney and the smoke billowed back into the room. So I lit the living-room fire and boiled a kettle and made toast there.

Jim came in, the breath completely knocked out of him on the short journey from the steading. One of the three giant rowans was up by the roots, he said, and the roof was off the henhouse, where we kept a small overflow of poultry. Sheets of corrugated iron were scattered over the near field and the cows' backs were powdered with fine snow, driven through minute cracks in the byre wall. Otherwise everything was all right!

We carried the woebegone hens bodily down to the byre and gave them a feed of corn. In the comparative warmth and shelter they soon revived and strutted happily among the cows' legs. Two of their mates were frozen stiff on the perches in the roofless house and we had to put them in the larder.

The rest of the day we spent huddled at the living-room fire, listening to the roar of the wind and the groaning of the house-beams, between trips to the steading. The deep-litter hens were completely unperturbed; they actually laid a record number of eggs that day. But Hope, the house-cow, didn't care at all for her coating of snow. We hastily stuffed every crevice in the byre wall with bits of sacking and wisps of straw. In the evening I stood, in complete outdoor rig, frying ham and eggs on a spirit-lamp in the ice-box of a kitchen, waiting for the crashing of the stove pipe on the iron roof.

Next day we heard on the wireless of the damage that the storm had done. Square miles of timber had been uprooted, square miles of coast flooded and scores of people made homeless. We had come off comparatively lightly in our little stone house on the bare hilltop.

By Monday evening everything was calm in the pale sunshine. We went the round of the sheep; they were all quite placidly grazing. We sawed some limbs off the fallen tree. Rowan logs burn well wet or dry, and we had a particularly bright fire that evening, but it was sad to see the flames licking the bark of this friendly old giant. On our next trip to town we saw hundreds more like him lying prone about the fields, their roots exposed, their huge crowns flattened against the earth. It was only then that we realised fully that it was indeed a hurricane we had survived. Being right in the centre of it, with immediate, practical problems to solve, we had not been aware at the time of the ferocity of the force let loose about our heads.

The terror of this day soon faded from our minds and we began to plan the spring campaign. We should have to tackle it on our own this year, as there was no source of casual labour in the district. Then it struck us—might there not be a student, somewhere in the city of Edinburgh, who would be glad to spend a few weeks working on a Highland croft, in the spring of the year, for his keep and pocket money? We had heard of various schemes whereby young people were sent to help on the small crofts in the west. They undertook such jobs as draining, peat-cutting and harvesting on a voluntary basis, in return for their keep. But they went, as a rule, to very small places which might fail utterly without help on account of the age or infirmity of their occupiers. Our place was not quite in that category! Still, we thought, we might apply privately for a student.

One night, when the wind was roaring about the house again, and the logs were hissing on the hearth and spring work seemed a hundred years away, we sat with a writing-pad between us and drew up a letter to the Secretary of the Students' Representative Council in Edinburgh. Between the sheltered quadrangle of the University and our few acres crouched against the hills a great gulf was certainly fixed. Would any student care to venture into these unknown wilds? we wondered.

We wrote a brief description of the place, the stock it carried and the work that was to be done. We offered to pay the rail fare and one pound a week pocket money to anyone who would live with us, as one of the family, and work from eight in the morning till about four in the afternoon. After that, his time was to be his own. He could do some reading, go out with the gun, or follow his fancy. If we had been students, we reflected, we should have jumped at the chance. We imagined there must still be a good few young men about the dusty classrooms who would be glad to give their lungs an airing and pit their wits against a fresh set of problems. We made no bones about it—the work would be hard, the food plain, and of streamlined entertainment there would be absolutely none.

With some misgiving we thought of a thin and pimply youth trying vainly to work out the intricacies of fitting Charlie to his harness, by a process of logical deduction, whereas the one thing needful, as a rule, is a bent nail, a length of stack rope or a kind word in his ear. Worse still, we thought, would be the embryo mathematician who would work out on squared paper the exact number of eggs we should be getting from each pullet if she were to justify her existence, bearing in mind the cost of feed, our own labour, overheads, etc. We might feel compelled to cull a quarter of our flock and, heaven knew, they might well come up to scratch yet if given a few weeks' grace! There are some things better left in the lap of the gods if each living hour is to keep its shine. And that was exactly where we left the procuring of our student help. If he were not a misfit, much mutual good might come of his stay. The Easter vacation, from mid-March to mid-April, should coincide, weather permitting, with our big rush of spring work. We posted our letter in hope and went on riding out the winter.

CHAPTER XII
SHINING MORNING FACE

THE larks were rising and falling in a blue, windless sky on the day Helen and I set off for Glen Convinth school. Lessons began at ten, so we left the house just after nine. Helen had her small, brown satchel on her back—it contained only a biscuit and an apple, but it looked quite impressive.

Bertha met us at the burn and we walked gaily. As we approached the school, three small girls came running to meet us. I recognised the bright faces and ringlets I had glimpsed through the open door a few weeks before. They were sisters, Bertha said. That was clear, for they were as like one another as three chickens. They immediately took charge of Helen, in a charming, motherly way, and she had vanished into the schoolroom before I'd even had time to say good-bye to her.

It had been arranged that I was to wait in the house where Mrs. Maclean's daughter lived, a stone's throw from the school, until the eleven o'clock play, when Helen and Bertha would come down to see me and report progress, before I set off for home. I was given tea and entertained with kindly talk. But still I couldn't help remembering my own unhappy beginnings in the schoolroom, and wondering how Helen was reacting to her strange surroundings.

I needn't have worried. At eleven o'clock, the two youngsters came rushing up the garden path and into the little parlour. Their eyes were bright and Bertha was as excited as an elder sister, as she proudly announced that Helen had got all her sums right!

Helen herself was quite overwhelmed by the attention of the motherly small girls and the thrill of all the new ploys she had embarked on.

At dusk we watched for the two small figures coming down the grassy slope. It had been a long day for a five-year-old, but when Helen came into the lamplight in the kitchen her cheeks were glowing and her eyes round as she recounted, in a few breathless snatches, the doings of the day.

Her schooldays had got off to a good start. She began to make progress at once, for her innate wish to learn was recognised and fostered. Her teacher, who had reared and taught four fine children of her own, knew instinctively the approach to make to a young, fresh mind.

The little classroom had none of the streamlined equipment deemed essential to the schooling of the modern infant. There were no glittering devices to allure young minds and make it seem that learning is some kind of glorified game. But there was something no large, impersonal classroom could achieve—the comfort of a relaxed atmosphere. The teacher didn't have to spend precious energy acting as a policewoman all the time. With only a handful of children confronting her, she found it comparatively easy to keep order, and she could give of her best to the actual job of teaching. Each child was known as an individual. His background was understood and thus his shortcomings could be accounted for and efforts to overcome them directed along the lines most likely to lead to success.

There was a homely feeling of security about the classroom itself. On bleak winter days the children found it a real refuge. Wet coats and boots were put to dry by the glowing stove, which was opened up for a few minutes to allow small, numb fingers to be rubbed in the warmth before lessons began. There were nice, friendly little customs; a new child had an older one to 'mother' her, to see that she put her things to dry, to accompany her on trips outside, to see that she washed her hands before dinner and that she made a good meal.

During the half-hour that Helen had to spend waiting for the bus, in the afternoon, while Bertha was still at her lessons in the 'big room', her teacher took her into the house and gave her tea and cake. On arrival at Mrs. Maclean's, she was again fortified with a hot drink and biscuits in winter, or lemonade in summer, so that the journey didn't seem wearisome or long. In fact, it was one gay adventure. Sometimes, after a day of torrential rain, the burn, which had been quite easily crossed in the morning, would be impassable by evening. Then Bertha would accompany Helen along to the road, over the bridge there and in through the gate at the 'west end'. We would hear the laughter rising above the roaring of the burn and we would see the torches weaving patterns in the dusk and we would go to meet the pair of them. Our own torch would reveal a couple of gleaming, laughing faces and we'd never catch a whimper of distress. Bertha would turn about for home and I would shepherd Helen into the kitchen, strip off her wet things and make her sit at the fire in her dressing-gown till she'd swallowed a cup of hot, sweet tea.

On spring evenings they'd dally all the way home, swinging their skipping ropes and stopping to examine the progress of the clutch of meadow-pipit's eggs in the tiny, neat nest in the bank by the well, or to watch the peewit fledgelings scurrying through the rushes, in their anxious mother's wake.

The following year, when Bertha had gone on to the Junior Secondary school, we would take it in turns to walk Helen to school in the mornings. For the return journey she still had Bertha's company from the school bus. We used to beguile the journey with the telling of a serial story, each of us, including Helen, taking it in turn to add our chapter. Jim usually managed to leave the protagonists in some fantastic predicament, from which I had to extricate them before Helen took over.

In these small country schools the children receive a thorough grounding in the basic disciplines, at a time when their minds can grasp first principles with amazing ease. This is important in an age when glamour seems to be invading even the infant classroom, and to 'have fun' seems to be the end of existence for too many young-sters. The healthy young imagination doesn't need much titillating, but the growing mind does need discipline. There are regular periods for drawing and singing, needlework and knitting for the girls, and handwork for the boys, but the main emphasis is on plain learning. In a very short time Helen was coming home, bristling with information in the fields of grammar, history and geography. 'Surely', we said, 'you're not doing that!' as we racked our brains to answer some question regarding the use of personal pronouns, or the place of embarkation of the Pilgrim Fathers. 'No', was the reply, 'but class four is.' We heard later from Bertha that Helen, when she had finished the task set her by the teacher, would sit wide-eyed and wide-eared, 'listening-in' to the lessons being given, in the same room, to another class.

These little schools are well supervised by the authorities. Inspectors pay them regular visits and a good standard is maintained. Most of the teachers and inspectors are people of Highland origin and have all the Highlander's respect for learning. There is nothing slap-dash about their attitude to letters. Doctor and dentist also pay regular visits. The nurse, who comes on a monthly tour of inspection, gets to know the children well. Medical examination holds no terror for them, as it has always been part of their routine.

The Education Authority is wisely keeping open the country schools, even when the number of pupils falls to as low as half a dozen. To transport the children to a bigger school, or even to a town school, would he comparatively simple. But once embark on that scheme and the depopulation of the remoter areas is assured. Up here, the boys would be happy as larks, tough, clear-eyed and skilled in country ploys, brought up to hard work, but getting an immense amount of fun out of a game of shinty, an afternoon's sledging, a day at the fox-drive. Come across them in town, and you find them lolling round Woolworth's, eating a bag of chips for their dinner, ogling a bunch of giggling girls, conforming to the inevitable pattern. They're soon ashamed of their old skills. To know how to thatch a rick, to snare a rabbit, to guddle trout has become for them the mark of the uncouth. Their one ambition is to 'come up on the pools', or find some other way to get rich quickly. Very soon, there's little to distinguish them from the town-bred youth of all the world.

It is a sad fact that in some of the remoter areas sheep flocks are disappearing, though there is greater need than ever of good, home-produced mutton and wool, because men cannot be found to undertake the shepherding. The skilled shepherd gets a good wage, a good house, good perquisites, everything necessary for a healthy, satisfying life, but he and his wife and family must be willing to live at a distance from the shops, the pub and the cinema. Apparently that is too much to ask of young people who have once had a taste of these things. So the 'Situations Vacant' column remains a long one, under the heading 'Agriculture', and only occasionally does one find a *cri du coeur* in the 'Situations Wanted'—'Young man wishes work on estate or farm. Remote area preferred.' Perhaps it is the voice crying in the urban wilderness, remembering the lost gods of hill and moor and sky.

There is no doubt that it is the willingness, or otherwise, of the female partner to embark on a lonely life, which can encourage or discourage a young man in the pursuit of a country career. A wise Education Authority has foreseen this, and in the Junior Secondary schools in the Highlands every effort is made to encourage the girls to be self-reliant and to take a pride in the old home crafts of cooking, laundering, needlework and child-care. There are several institutions, actually in the Highlands, where young women can be trained as instructresses in these crafts, without having to go near an urban centre.

Scotland is not a country of great natural resources. Her contribution to the world is all the greater because of that bare fact. Her contribution lies in the character of her people, which has been tempered in the struggle to make the most of what resources the land can yield. A man will easily grow fat when the ripe fruit falls into his mouth as he lies in the shade of the tree. But when he has to plough the soil a few inches deep on a rocky hill-side before his little crop of oats will blossom, if blossom is the word, then he'll have to grow tough and skilled and resilient, or perish—and the Scot has no notion to perish. He loves his rocky hillside with the fierce passion of a man for a woman who will not easily yield.

Scotland today is becoming more and more industrialised. The Scots character, after a generation or two, is swallowed up in the standardisation imposed by an urban way of life. The remote areas remain the breeding-ground of the country's most precious asset —character. Only there can the Scot remain completely true to himself, for that is where he is rooted. Other countries, other parts, have exploited his abilities for long enough. When he comes home, in his dapper suit, his Stetson and his rimless glasses, to grasp his brother's rough hand again, he is looking for something. His pockets may be brimful, but he has learnt, in his canny way, that money imposes its own tyranny. He is no longer independent in the old, satisfying way.

Why is it that the influx of exiled Scots, come to take another look at the country of their origin, grows steadily greater every year? It's because, at bottom, every Scot recognises the validity of the old human virtues. You can't fob him off with make-believe. He doesn't live easily in a climate of success, he must have something to get his teeth into. He was always happiest ploughing his few inches on the rock, or sailing his boat smack into the wind. He'll work all the hours there are, tending his own few acres and his stock, but give him an assured job and he's the worst clockwatcher in the world.

We have a neighbour, thin as a wraith and crippled with old wounds. It is a greater miracle each year how he gets his crop gathered and a fresh one down in spring. But he must be working about his fields, or there would be no cheery twinkle in his eye, no witty word of greeting as he meets us on the road. When he mangled his hand in his barn mill, he would walk the two miles to the bus to go into town for daily treatment as an out-patient rather than spend a week in hospital, as the doctors recommended. He had his beasts to see to, and his independence to preserve. It will be a bad day for the world when toughness like his has been destroyed by the palliatives of a welfare state. The best way to keep alive is to be constantly at grips with one's universe.

One evening in early March we were sitting quietly at the fire when Billy burst into the kitchen, wide-eyed, a little scared-looking. 'The hill's on fire', he announced, 'we were afraid the van might get it!' We rushed to the window on the other side of the house; the whole of the southern sky was glowing orange. The Macleans, whose house faces the hill, had evidently been watching the advance of the flames and had sent Billy to warn us. We flung on our coats and boots and made for the spot where the van was standing. True enough, the flames were within a few yards of it and, though the road lay between, the rising wind might easily carry a spark across the narrow safety belt. We moved the van as far as possible out of harm's way and began beating out the flames along the roadside, but within minutes the thing was hopelessly out of control. We could only stand listening to the terrifying roar and crackle and hope that the wind would die before morning.

After an hour or so of fruitless efforts to control even the burning of the rushes at the roadside, we went back to the house. From the upper windows we could see the full extent of the fearsome blaze. By morning it had died down considerably, but was still burning here and there. Luckily the sheep were out of harm's way and the fencing on the eastern boundary had escaped damage. It was a warning to us for future heather-burning operations of our own. Once again we were thankful for the Macleans' vigilance and goodwill.

The smell of heather burning and the sight of plovers swooping over the fields, in the cold, afternoon light, make the reality of an upland spring. We've seen small tokens of a change in things from mid-February, perhaps—a softening in the light that pours down the hill-side from the peak of the noonday sun, the sudden, unlooked-for blooming of a daisy or a coltsfoot in a sheltered hollow by the burn. But the burning of the old heather and the wild agitation of the returning birds mean that things are really happening—space is being sought for new life and growth.

The first new arrivals in our own spring season came in small cardboard boxes from hundreds of miles away—a batch of day-old chickens all the way from Dumfriesshire. Train and bus had brought them to the foot of the hill, the post's motor-bike pillion conveyed them to our door. When we opened the boxes on the kitchen table, it seemed a miracle that these small, yellow, chirping atoms had safely and cheerfully survived such a journey on the day of their birth. We installed them, with two brooder lamps, in the glasshouse and they throve wonderfully well; we lost only three out of a batch of one hundred.

We presented a broody hen with a dozen day-old Aylesbury ducklings. She took to them at once, and they to her. They grew so fast that, within days, she had difficulty in keeping them covered. Finally she gave up the attempt and would strut after them, with much exasperated clucking, as they waddled off, in a determined line, to seek their own kind of fortune among the damp rushes. A few weeks later we took them in a crate to the butcher. They went to grace the tables of the more expensive Inverness hotels. They were lovable, comical things and we missed the sight of them about the place. I doubt if we shall ever acquire the complete detachment of the man who makes rearing for the market his business.

CHAPTER XIII
'GAUDEAMUS IGITUR'

WE had one reply to our request for a student to help during the Easter vacation. One, out of all the hundreds who must have seen the small notice pinned on the board in the University quadrangle, had had the courage to take at least a tentative step towards our fastness! He was a veterinary student, which sounded promising, John by name. We answered his letter hopefully, and it was arranged that he would come in the middle of March.

No sooner was this plan fixed than we heard from an Arts student, Henry, who sounded very enthusiastic. We hated to turn him down; perhaps two students would be better than one, we thought. They would keep each other company and that might make for a happy atmosphere. Besides, one never knew, the first one might fall by the way. So we offered to engage Henry as well as John. However, we received no acknowledgement of our letter to Henry, so we concluded he would not be coming.

As the day of John's arrival drew near, I managed, between thrice-daily trips to the chickens and bouts of liming and digging the garden plot, to get a room ready for him. It was bare enough, but it had the elements of simple comfort. We guessed that a young man who would venture, in mid-March, to a spot one thousand feet above sea-level would not be too fussy.

The day we were expecting John, a wire came saying that Henry was due at Inverness station the following afternoon! That was a hectic day by any standard. We had been over to say good-bye to Willie Maclean, who was going into hospital. We were behind with the work, and I had a baking to do for the extra mouth we were expecting, and now it seemed we had to expect two after all.

Still, the evenings were lengthening. After tea, we harnessed Charlie and brought a spare bed along from the bungalow. Bertha came over to give a hand—Mrs. Maclean must have guessed we had a crisis on hand. We set the mattress and blankets to air, we collected odds and ends of furnishings from all over the house, and, by the time Jim returned from the station with John, Henry's room was ready and I was able to welcome our guest with a calm which quite belied the storm that had been raging all day.

We took to John at once. He wore corduroys and carried his gear in a rucksack. He was tall and quiet and looked as though he wouldn't easily be defeated. He confessed right away that he'd never worked with a horse, but said he could drive a car and was sure he could manage the tractor.

Next day we went to meet the three-thirty-four train. After unsuccessfully accosting several young men, who looked as if they might have come north for a working holiday, we finally ran Henry to earth at the very end of the stream of passengers. He was dark, twinkling and dapper and he was struggling with a heavy suitcase. A more complete contrast to John could not be imagined; Henry hardly ever stopped talking or laughing. But after a day or two the five of us settled into a pleasant enough routine.

The weather was superb. After dispelling the morning mist the sun rose, day after day, into a sky of sheer, summer blue. The larks were singing, the peewits flashing, the curlews gliding over the moor. I think John quietly revelled in the freshness and Henry, who was a good deal older and had knocked a bit about the world, couldn't help feeling a touch of the magic. John soon learnt to harness and drive Charlie; he took to the field-work at once. In a battered old tweed hat and jacket he'd stride about the place, taking things calmly, as a countryman does. Henry, on the other hand, couldn't quite adjust himself to the tempo of the land, and he always managed to look dapper. He'd make the most extraordinary noises of encouragement to Charlie, as though they were both something out of a circus. But Henry was certainly anxious to be helpful. One very stormy day he offered to feed the hens for me. I gladly accepted and gave him the pail of mash. But my heart nearly stood still as I heard the terrified flutterings and squawkings issuing from the hen-house. Henry's imitation of a mother-hen was enough, had he only known it, to put any self-respecting pullet off the lay for several days!

Helen enjoyed the boys' stay immensely. After supper, Henry would set her problems in arithmetic, or do a drawing for her, or make wonderful models out of plasticine.

The boys could certainly work. They spread cartfuls of lime and manure; they scythed rushes; they helped to dip the sheep. And they were ready to deal with any emergency. After the first ten days or so of superb, unbelievable spring weather, we had two or three days of real storm. The water came swirling off the slope of the moor and began to seep into the glass-house, where the chickens were. The boys set to with spades and deepened the trench round the glass-house before the chickens were engulfed. They enjoyed this battle with the elements. We could hardly dissuade Henry, after that, from digging drains; so great was his enthusiasm that he drew up a plan for draining the whole moor. We had to explain that, much as we should have liked to embark on some such scheme, we had to submit to the pressure of other work. When you're running a small place on your own, you hardly ever manage to catch up with the bare essentials, let alone undertake the more grandiose projects—it's always a case of 'next year' for the big things. So Henry had to be dragged from his draining to spread muck on the potato ground.

I was kept hard at work, during those spring weeks, coping with the boys' appetites. Well I remembered how we had been perpetually hungry in our first months in the hills. After a day or two working in the keen air, there was a gleam in the boys' eyes as they came into the kitchen at meal times. Henry would quite openly sniff the warm smell coming from the oven and rub his hands with satisfaction as he sat down. John would just murmur, 'That Irish stew's good. Funny... I'd never look at it in the canteen, but here...' I knew what that 'here' meant. The vitalising effect of satisfying work in the high air was working its spell. As I heaped John's plate, I glanced at his face. The pale, rather haunted look of the student had gone, I noticed, and there was a hint of the countryman's weathered confidence about his features. Perhaps our scheme *was* having the two-way effect we had hoped for.

The boys were to have one day in the week completely free. On their first holiday they both went to Inverness. But after that they put sandwiches in their pockets and had a long day in the hills. In their free time, after five o'clock, they never once opened a text-book; but they climbed the near hills, they went over the moor with the gun, they called on various families in the district and were made welcome in Highland style.

John, as a veterinary student, was naturally interested chiefly in the animals. I think he was genuinely sorry that his spell with us would be over before lambing started. I'm sure he would have settled quite happily, at any time, into a hill-man's life. Henry, on the other hand, never quite accepted his sense of isolation. He was inclined to want to post letters, send wires, or make telephone calls at all sorts of odd moments. He had the townsman's attitude to living arrangements. Milk came out of a bottle, water out of a tap, and that was that. It never occurred to him to wonder how it was that water did, in fact, come out of a tap, in this wilderness. The result was that he would let the water run while shaving, till the cistern was emptied and the household threatened with drought until it had time to fill up again. Poor Henry! He couldn't quite understand the maledictions that descended on his good-natured head! Perhaps only those who've carried water in pails, dragged logs from the wood and sawn them, can fully appreciate the value of the simple necessities—water and fire.

Towards the end of the month, John had a shot at ploughing the field we were to bring into cultivation that year. The boys had scythed the rushes that were choking it, they'd removed several large boulders, and now it was ready for ploughing. John did very well. We called the field 'John's field' and we sowed it later with oats and grass seed. When John came to see us, several years later, he cast a reminiscent eye over it. It had obviously been quite often in his thoughts. The day the boys were due to leave, John's father and sister arrived to fetch him. They had come north by car, for a long weekend, and were picking him up on their way home. We were all out finishing off a job in the yard when they arrived. It was a typical spring day of sudden squalls and gleams of sunlight. Mr. S., getting no answer to his knock at the door, rounded the gable of the house, clutched his hat as a gust of wind nearly carried it off, caught sight of us and roared, 'You don't really *live* here, do you?'

I'm afraid that is the reaction of quite a lot of chance visitors to our small domain. By the time they have found the place on the map (large-scale), been directed by several neighbours, with varying degrees of explicitness, have drawn the car into the side of the narrow road, taken the path through the heather, climbed the stile and pushed open the garden gate (which is always so well barricaded against marauding cattle, that it's sometimes easier to climb the fence, anyway), there is generally an expression of blank dismay on their faces. We have come to know it well, but we have our defences ready. A chair drawn up to a blazing fire, a cup of steaming tea and a plateful of well-buttered scones will usually work wonders in winter or spring. In summer or autumn, a dish of fruit and cream and a stroll out on to the moor will generally do the trick.

Perhaps the most enthusiastic visitors we have ever had were two young Norwegians, man and wife. They stayed a week with us in very stormy weather, one October, and they loved every moment of their stay. It was just like home, they said. The only thing that surprised them was that we allowed the sheep to roam the hills all winter. In Norway they have to be brought into shelter and hand-fed for months. Some of the most 'marginal' of our land would be considered, they said, quite first-class in parts of Norway, where soil is so precious, and the fields have actually to be built before anything can be grown. The deep-litter system of poultry-keeping intrigued them greatly.

The very day after the boys' departure, the lambs began to arrive. There was half a gale blowing as we staggered round the moor, looking for the tiny white specks. Over the following days, it rained, it snowed, it blew, and the lambs kept on appearing. We wished John were there to help. Mercifully, no mishap occurred, though it was the kind of pitiless, harsh weather that is very hard on a new-born lamb.

Towards the end of April we decided to sell 'Red Mary', the cross-Highland cow. She had always been a bit of a terror. Having bigger and better horns than any of the other cows, she had become a bully, and her athletic powers had increased over the years. She could jump, if not over the moon, at least over the highest fence we could manage to erect. Any fence she didn't feel like jumping she would persistently lean against at a weak spot until it gave way, when she would step elegantly over, inviting the other cows, with a toss of her head, to follow. We felt we couldn't put up with her tricks for another growing season. Already, the year before, Jim had had to take to sleeping with his bed jammed against the window, so that he could look out at first light to see what marauders were in the crops. Many a morning he had gone out in pyjamas and gum-boots, to drive Red Mary out of the springing corn.

It was a bitter morning of snow, and blowing hard, when Jim went to take Red Mary to the fank to await the cattle float. I decided to keep Helen at home, for the moor road looked most uninviting. Jim had been gone a full hour and I was plodding round the yard, seeing to the hens, wondering when the float would arrive, when I saw Alec and a Forestry man coming down the path from the stile. 'Have you a ladder?' Alec asked. 'Why, yes, I think so.' One is never surprised at being asked for anything up here, but I did find the ladder puzzling, and Alec's manner was a little strange.

'It's Jim', he went on, 'He's not bad, really, but... the heifer dragged him, he...' My heart began to jump.

'The heifer dragged him...' That wretched Red Mary! He'd had her on the rope, she'd been determined to break free, Jim had been equally determined that she wouldn't. He'd held on firmly and she'd dragged him for yards along the road. I stopped trying to picture what might have happened and found a short ladder. I took a rug and followed the men to where Jim was lying at the roadside. No bones were broken, but he was sick and his face was the most ghastly shade of green, with a mauve tinge round the mouth. Alec and the Forestry man carried him to the house on the improvised stretcher. We pulled off his boots and lifted him into bed, then I smothered him with blankets and hot-water bottles. I persuaded him to drink a cup of sweet, hot tea and we left him to lie quiet.

Alec promised to see to all the cows for me. Nellie, our easterly neighbour, came to offer to take charge of Helen if I wanted to go for the doctor, but Jim wouldn't hear of this. Duncan went the lambing round. As ever, we felt surrounded with goodwill. I got a fire going and slipped in to see Jim every half-hour. He was sleeping peacefully and I was thankful to see that his face was its normal colour. By tea-time he was sitting up, eating a boiled egg. I could hardly persuade him to stay in bed until the following morning. 'That darned heifer', he muttered, at regular intervals. She was, alas, still with us, for the snow had deterred the float from coming. As I looked out into the dusk, I could see her doing her best to resist Alec's efforts to get her into the byre for the night.

April had been, as it most often is, a cruel month, though March had been so lovely. But we managed to get the corn and the grass-seed sown. Come what may, seed-time and harvest are always somehow or other achieved. I think it will always remain a bit of a miracle to us that this is so, perhaps because we were not actually born to face the odds of hill-top farming. To the native hill-man it is just in the nature of things that there should be endless difficulties to overcome. If everything went smoothly, he would be inclined to suspect a catch. To us, the wonder is that the stacks still rise against the skyline each autumn, though it may be November before the last ones appear, that the beasts thrive, the little chimneys have each their plume of smoke and the men and women smile a welcome, inevitably, in the doorways.

Towards the beginning of May, when the weather was beginning to relent, we heard disquieting news from over the burn. Willie Maclean was home from hospital and his wife was hoping he would soon be able to get a breath of the soft air. What he needed was to sit on the seat at the gable of the little house and feel the sun warm on his face and hands, she said. But Willie couldn't pick up strength to walk that far; he could only sit in his room and talk in quiet snatches and make plans for his wife and his household. He had got very thin and weak. The doctor could do nothing for him, and one Sunday night he slipped away.

The minister held a service in the house on the Tuesday evening; on the Wednesday was the funeral. Jim was asked to help at the graveside. We were deeply touched by this gesture and we were proud to think we had been his friends. The children and young people of his and of his daughter's house spent the day of the funeral with Helen and me. From the window we heard the cadences of the Gaelic hymns rising and falling in the still air. We watched the long procession of men following Willie to his rest. It is sad when a man like Willie goes, for there are none to take his place. Willie could work his fields, talk of history and poetry in the Gaelic and the English idioms, slate a roof, play the pipes, and keep a secure home for his family. He was a man deeply rooted, complete in himself. Men don't seem to grow to that wholeness now.

When the last of the potatoes were in and the garden planted, and while we were waiting for a little rain to moisten the ground before sowing the turnip seed, I started the spring cleaning. It was the first really big one I had tackled, for hitherto the house had nearly always been in some state of upheaval and thorough cleaning had been done piecemeal, as each room came into use. Now, however, we were more or less settled, our living had fallen into a pattern. Most modern housewives would shudder at the amount of sheer brute force needed for a croft cleaning—there are no shortcuts.

Jim gave me a hand to carry the upholstered chairs and the carpets out on to the grass, where I beat them till the dust flew away in clouds. I washed the blankets and draped them on the bushes in the sun. Curtains and paintwork keep very clean in the hills, for there is no grime to encrust them. Only the living-room and the kitchen really needed much in the way of hard scrubbing. Oil-lamps certainly make ceilings black. Kitchens which are used for every conceivable purpose—and may have to be converted at a moment's notice into hospitals for sick lambs and chickens, or (on occasions, when the outside boiler breaks down) into cookhouses for pigs—can do with any amount of cleaning. But I really enjoyed this hard work. After the long, dark winter, when damp seeps into the corners, it's good to be able to set doors and windows wide and to feel the warm, scented air flowing through the house.

The Highland crofter-wife takes a great pride in freshening her house every May-time. The fabric of her dwelling may not be all that could be desired. In many cases the rooms are unlined, just 'plastered on the hard', but she makes tremendous efforts to keep the place neat and cosy, against appalling odds. She has no water laid on, her fire is an open range, her light an oil-lamp or a candle. Yet every spring she repapers one or more rooms, she distempers her kitchen ceiling, she paints her doors and window-frames. As long as she keeps a gay flag flying there will still be life in the hills. She is well aware of all the devices of the day for making the house-wife's lot an easier one. Has not her daughter, who's married to a townsman, a pressure-cooker and a washing-machine? She doesn't hanker miserably for these things, any more than her daughter might hanker for a trip to the moon. But the wise crofter is the one who, on getting a good price for his stirks at the autumn sales, brings home a boiling-ring run on bottled gas, or a pressurised oil-heater for the bedroom. These things do help.

Every croft house has its small flower patch by the door. It is difficult enough some years, goodness knows, to get even the crops to grow, and a little kail for the soup-pot. But it is only an abandoned dwelling that hasn't its little bush of roses:

'...the little white rose of Scotland
That smells sharp and sweet—and breaks the heart',

its few pansies or marigolds, to greet the sun. Summer must be made the most of, must be received with at least a touch of ceremonial. That is why the croft-wife thumps her mats and hangs them in the sweet air with such glad enthusiasm. Her life still keeps time with the natural swing of the universe. In a centrally heated, hygienically contrived flat, equipped with every labour-saving device, there is no real need of a special turn-out in spring. No doubt it is at all times in almost immaculate state, and spring-cleaning has become little more than an accepted custom. For the small house in the hills, it's as though it were putting out fresh leaf and bud, as the heather does in May.

CHAPTER XIV
A DINNER OF HERBS

THE sixteenth of June was a red-letter day in the life of the community. It was the day our bus service to Inverness was started. Once a week, on Tuesday (market day), the small, red-and-yellow bus was to come nosing its way up the long, twisting hill to a point just above the school, where it would turn and await its passengers. The Caiplich folk had a mile or more to walk before joining it, and some would harness up the pony and 'machine' for this part of the journey. The bus went off at eight-thirty in the morning and left Inverness again at three in the afternoon. Later, the time of departure was put on to ten-fifteen, so as to give the women-folk time to get the morning work done. It was impossible, at any rate in winter, to get the cow milked, the hens fed, the children off to school, dinner put ready for those left behind, and oneself changed by eight-fifteen, or earlier. So now we leave in a state of composure at the back of ten and are home again at six-thirty.

These are changed days, indeed, for the women who remember having to be at the pier at Loch Ness-side at eight in the morning, or else having to jolt all the twelve miles behind a tired pony: and for the men who remember walking home on market night, sometimes through chest-high drifts of snow, when they'd come across old friends and had missed the steamer!

There are people still not past middle-age who tell of mothers and aunts walking to Inverness with a great basket of eggs on their arm, which they would sell in order to buy scraps of comfort for their families. Now, the egg-van passes every gate weekly and leaves his price in a neat envelope. Of course, fifty years ago the croft produced practically all the simple necessities of hard living. The oats were ground at the mill, which still stands today, and were made into brose, porridge and bannocks. The cow gave milk, butter and crowdie, the fields potatoes and turnips, the garden patch kail and cabbage. The rabbit made a tasty, nourishing stew. Whisky itself, the water of life, was made locally by those with skill and daring! In autumn the men from several neighbouring crofts would set off with the horse and cart to fetch a barrel of salt herring from the west—and a fine holiday jaunt they made of it! There was a lot of honest-to-goodness happiness about in those days. Those who could afford to do so would pickle a sheep or a pig for winter eating. Each district had its own shoemaker and sometimes its own tailor. These would often give of their skill in return for a service or a load of peats from the hill. In a countryside where practically every family bears the same surname, it is essential to have some distinguishing mark and the old trade names come in handy. This is Fraser country. We can easily tell which Fraser we are talking about, for one will be 'the tailor', one 'the shoemaker', one 'the mason', or else it will be the name of his place we shall use— Rinudin, or Corry-foyness, or Ladycairn. A money economy has taken the place of the old self-sufficiency. The crofter now sells all he can for cash, even his surplus potatoes and a few bags of oats; and spending facilities are not lacking. In addition to the grocer's weekly visit, we have a call a week from the Cooperative travelling shop and two from an Inverness butcher. But the old communal independence and self-reliance are still strong. The exchange of goods and services between neighbours is looked on as part of the natural scheme of living. The handling of money still comes awkwardly to gnarled fingers and the older Highland mind still assesses things in terms of their actual value in the fostering of life. A load of peats will warm his house; tatties, eggs and milk will feed the bairns; a stack of corn will keep cattle, horse and hens in good heart for many a winter week; whereas money just seems to slip away, leaving no trace.

The crofter still doesn't quite believe in the Welfare State. He's glad enough of his pension, of course, when it comes, and of the doctor's services, should they be needed. But he has always had his own welfare assured by his own community. Should he fall sick, he knows that his neighbour will see to his cattle and his crops as though they were his own. Should his wife be ill, his neighbour's wife will come morning and evening to look after his household.

He would always rather be aloof from outside interference, and is even a little wary of it, however well it may be meant. And who can blame him? In the past, Government measures have done him little good. In fact, the reverse has most often been the case. After the breakdown of the clan system, which had its measure of security, and the arrival of the moneyed, absentee landlord, who sanctioned evictions of a most barbarous nature, the crofter felt lost and bewildered. Is it any wonder, when his roof was burnt about his head and he and his family were 'compensated' with a strip of shelterless bogland? The old feeling of resentment against an alien authority dies hard. Human dignity, when ambushed, takes many a queer twist but, thanks be, it is the last thing to perish in the hills. The authorities find the crofter hard to regiment, he exasperates officialdom, but his sheer doggedness has carried him through. At last, with the passing of the Crofters' Act of 1955 and the establishment of the new Commission, with a man of imagination born of crofting stock at its head, the crofter is beginning to feel his way back to a real status.

In an over-industrialised world where all sorts of artificial supplies clamour to create artificial demands, the validity of the crofter's way of life may be in doubt. Has any man the right to go on quietly cultivating his small fields, rearing his beasts, meeting most of his own needs, and thriving into the bargain? Is he not a bit of an anachronism? How can he be catered for in a world where the cash nexus is supreme? Ought he not to be cutting out his neighbour, sharpening his wits, striving to capture new markets, making money surplus to his requirements, so that he can buy the television sets, the labour-saving gadgets, the patent medicines which every man alive is supposed to need so urgently? In the name of progress, what is he doing, all alone on his plot of wilderness? He's simply minding his own business, working his own hours, keeping a clear head and a stomach free of ulcers, that's all. And, heaven knows, that is a major achievement for an industrial slave, be he machine-minder or company director these days. A country suffering from the effects of a top-heavy economic regime, now looks to the crofter to produce one extra carcass of beef and mutton, one extra box of eggs, so that his place in the scheme of things may be justified.

As the summer wore on we began to wish, more fervently than we had ever wished for anything, that we had been born to croft-ing ways. Our notion of what was essential for a good working life was still affected by our urban background. We had never been really 'up against it', as the crofter has, most of the time. We had spent nothing on luxuries, but when we needed an implement we bought it instead of making do with a substitute. The tractor, though it had done much useful pioneering work in our early days, we now found was a continual drain on our resources. The cost of running it was out of proportion to the benefits it bestowed. We should have done better to have made use of the Government tractor service for the big operations and relied on the horse for light work. We had never imagined we could have become as adept as we actually had in managing Charlie and the horse-drawn implements.

We decided to sell most of our mechanical contraptions and with the proceeds from them increase our stock. The sheep were beginning to show a return. They produce two crops a year— wool and lambs, but we hadn't room for more than we were carrying. Cattle are slow to give a return; they are two or three years a-growing and nine months a-breeding and a hard winter can so easily set them back. Our fattening pigs had done well and had given Jim a definite leaning towards a piggery. We had a sound spare barn along at the far steading. A good sow can produce two litters of up to a dozen piglets a year, and the market was good. So it came about that on the fourteenth of July three Large White in-pig gilts were delivered to us by float.

They were magnificent creatures. Alec came along to see them the following day. He stood, slowly shaking his head and murmuring, 'What pigs, what pigs! I never saw the like!' Neither had we. They were so pink and white and massive and self-assured, the very cream of the pig aristocracy. We felt we ought to apologise to them for the bareness of their new surroundings, for the quality of the feeding we had to offer. To scratch their backs and murmur 'porky, porky!' into their pink, transparent ears seemed like sacrilege.

A week after their arrival, one of them produced seven piglets. A few days later, another had a litter of fourteen, two of which died at birth, and then the third produced a small litter of five. Every spare moment found us leaning over the side of the pens, gazing at these twenty-four small, squirming youngsters. A lot depended on them. We had had to buy in some expensive feeding to keep their mothers in good trim, and we were overdrawn at the bank to the limit the banker could allow. If the pigs could bring us in a quick return, which would carry us on till the sheep and cattle really began to show a substantial profit, our vital corner would be turned. We were in our tricky year, and at the trickiest part of it. Spending money was short, as the hens were in their seasonal decline and the new pullets would not be in production for another two or three months. We cut down expenses to the bone, literally to the bone! Instead of buying a small pot roast, or stewing mutton, I went hunting for the beefiest-looking bones at the butcher's and made potfuls of good soup with the tender garden vegetables. Milk could be turned into an endless variety of dishes, and eggs and cheese gave us most of our solid protein.

The pigs made a lot of work, for their quarters had to be cleaned out daily and the potatoes that eked out their expensive rations had to be boiled. But they and their offspring throve. After a few weeks, we moved them out into home-made arks on the heather, and it was rewarding to see them revelling in the sun and air. Slowly we began to gain confidence in the pig plan. Billy had left school and was spending nearly all his time helping us. We decided to put the thing on a business footing by paying him a small weekly wage, which we managed to squeeze, somehow, out of the housekeeping money. He certainly justified his keep, for he worked the same hours as we did ourselves. It was sometimes difficult to persuade him to go home. Even on Sunday mornings, he would come over to feed the pigs, so that Jim could take it easier. After breakfast he would potter about, or go for a sheep that had strayed, or tinker with implements in the barn. In his own young, only half-articulate way he was quietly yet stubbornly determined to make a life on his own terms.

The grass was cut by the man from 'the Board' that year. The weather was very mixed and we had a lot of heartbreak before the hay was made. It had to be turned and turned again, hung on the fences to dry and left out in small coils in the fields for weeks. But what nearly broke our backs, as well as our hearts, was the turnip crop. The field was one of the worst on the place, it had only had a scant harrowing in spring, owing to pressure of other work, and the tilth was not nearly fine enough. Through lack of moisture the seed had taken a long time to germinate and the weeds, which, apparently, nothing will deter, had shot ahead of the tiny seedlings. By the time these were ready for singling, they were engulfed in a mass of flourishing vegetation of every obnoxious kind. We slashed and battered at the drills, till every muscle in our bodies was stiff and aching. At the end of it all, we had about half a crop to show for our labours. I think the punishment I should choose for my worst enemy would be a few weeks singling turnips in a field strewn with sods and boulders, and with weeds leering maliciously from every drill!

The nightmare of the hay and turnips was hardly over, when it was time to cut the corn. Jim and Billy had only just time to make the roads before the Board tractor came chugging into the field. No sooner was the cutting done than the rain came down in torrents. There are few jobs as depressing as setting wet sheaves in stook. No protective clothing can keep you really dry; the rain pours off your coat, seeps down the back of your neck and into your boots. As you lift the sheaves, the water runs up your sleeves and soaks you to the elbow. That was altogether a depressing harvest.

We began to cast about for ways and means of making a little ready cash. There were quite a few grouse about, on our ground, but we never had time to go after them with the gun. We had heard fascinating tales of how the crofters used to leave a few stooks out in the field, long after harvest, and set them with snares, to catch the grouse. The town butcher relied on the 'parcels' smuggled in to him, along with an old boiling fowl from the back of the crofter's cart. We soon learnt to make the nooses of fine wire and to fix them on the stooks and every morning we would go out early to look for our catch. We got about a dozen birds in this way and took them hopefully to the butcher, on our next trip to town, but he gave us very little for them. No doubt many moors are commercialised now, and the shops are well stocked. We were only sorry we had not put the carcasses into our own oven.

The lambs were a poorer lot that year and didn't look as though they would make more than moderate prices. We knew that we couldn't expect things to go our way all the time, but we would have given a lot for a lift during those anxious weeks. We had come to have a liking for life in the hills that amounted almost to a passion and the thought of having to abandon it was intolerable. We must, we resolved, find some way of getting round our difficulties.

In mid-September a new arrival came along to take our minds off our worries. A new face about the place always cheers one up. The livestock marketing people, who had helped us over the buying of the gilts, agreed to let us have a boar, on the 'never-never', that is, we put a small sum down and undertook to pay the rest of the purchase price when the piglets were sold. These arrangements are disarmingly simple when entered into. With a few nods and smiles and flourishes of the pen, the bargain was made and McFlannel was among us.

There was no other name we could have given him. He was a good deal smaller than his intendeds and hadn't a trace of pomposity about him. He was quite unspoilt, cheerful and anxious to please. We housed him in an ark, in a field of his own, where he settled quite contentedly. He made overtures through the fence to a few inquiring sheep and he had no objection to the hens joining him in his feed of slops. He was altogether a much more lovable creature than the haughty, pampered members of his harem. They, however, did agree to consort with him at the appropriate time and thus, we hoped, another generation of piglets was assured.

Meanwhile, things were not going too well in the pig trade and prices were falling. It certainly began to look as though we had entered the field too late, as there had been over-production and a glut was threatening. About the middle of October we decided to sell one piglet to test the market. He was a nice, compact little fellow, obviously off well-bred stock, and we felt quite proud of him when we saw him in his market pen and compared him with others on offer. He fetched ten pounds. It was quite a good price, in the state the market was in and, a fortnight later, we got another lot of piglets ready for sale.

The float was late in coming to fetch them; that is the price one has to pay for living in the remoter areas. The float-hirers always leave the difficult places to the last. They would rather avoid them altogether, if they could, and they all have an aversion to loading pigs. The result was that our lot did not reach the market until the sale was almost over. They looked wretched, having been cooped up for hours, and they made very disappointing prices. We decided to take the remaining pigs in individually in the van, but by this time there was a real landslide in prices. The day we took one on our own demand was exceptionally slow, and we brought him home again rather than let him go for a song.

Then, about a week before Christmas, poor old McFlannel fell ill. The male of any species is never anything like as tough as the female. We laid him on a stretcher of planks and carried him, inch by inch, to a warm place in a corner of the byre, where we made him a deep bed of straw and then sent for the vet. He diagnosed pneumonia. Next day, McFlannel died. Billy was nearer to tears than I have ever seen him; I think he had a real affection for McFlannel. We buried him with heavy hearts. His widows looked flourishing enough, but we took extra care of them, just in case. A lot depended on their bringing forth McFlannel's offspring safely, in the New Year.

CHAPTER XV
WE WEAR THE GREEN WILLOW

ONE day early in January Jim, Billy and I were clearing mud from the yard. The weather had been mild and the accumulation of squelch was such that one was liable to leave a gum-boot behind in it on one's journey to the steading. Charlie stood patiently, while we filled the cart over and over again with the heavy, gluey muck. There can be a touch of magic in a winter afternoon, but that particular one hadn't a glimmer about it. The sky was overcast. The pigs and pullets looked dejectedly out from the mesh doors of their dwellings. We were spattered with mud from head to foot, our backs and arms were aching, and still the wretched stuff never seemed to get any less. Yet the strange thing was we were perfectly happy. I caught Jim's eye: suddenly, for no reason that we could think of, we found ourselves chuckling!

In a flash it came to me—might not people who were forced to spend their working hours between walls like to hear about what went on in a hill-top croft, of how it was possible to get an immense amount of fun and satisfaction out of lifting loads of mud into a cart, even though your boots were leaking and you knew there was not enough in the kitty to buy another pair? Would they like to know about the way light could stream down a blue hillside on a spring noon, how a lark could suddenly leap into a pale, washed sky after a night of storm and make the air ring with song, of how it was possible to get by every sort of difficulty as long as there was this knowledge that you were all in it together, this solidarity with rock and sun and bird? I believed they would.

The next afternoon when everything, including ourselves, was fed and I had a couple of hours to spare before going to meet Helen at the burn, I sat down at the kitchen table and wrote a short piece about the stillness of January in the hills, about the satisfaction of keeping the animals tended and biding one's time till the earth swung round to the sun again, about the small thrill of seeing the child of the house come safely home into the lamplight each evening, her cheeks glowing with the frosty air. The writing came easily, for I was talking about the things our days were made of. I had always liked writing, though I had only had an odd story or two published many years before. Luckily, I still had my old typewriter.

The next evening I typed my sketch, attached a snapshot of the croft and sent it to the editor of a Glasgow paper. In Glasgow, I thought, there must be many Highland exiles, who might like to read about the life they had once known at first hand. The typescript was back within the week, with a polite letter from the editor explaining about shortage of space and so on.

I posted it to the editor of the *Weekly Scotsman*. A few days later, back came the large return envelope I had enclosed. I took it from the post and had my usual chat with him about the weather and the doings of the day. I opened the other communications he had brought—a couple of bills, a circular and a Government form. I picked up the 'reject' envelope and was about to toss it on to the dresser with the others, when it struck me that it was surprisingly thin. I held it up to the light. There was certainly no typescript inside. I tore it open and drew out a single sheet of paper. It was a letter from the editor, thanking me warmly for the article and the photograph, which he proposed to use in his next issue, and indicating that he would like me to send one every month, for a trial period! I opened the door and called to Jim. He came into the kitchen and took the letter in his muddy fingers and we looked at each other with disbelieving eyes.

Before the end of the month the article appeared, along with the picture of our house. I have gone on writing these little articles ever since, and I have found each one a pleasure to do. They have brought us friends from places as far apart as Texas and Australia.

The kindly welcome given to my effort by the editor of the *Weekly Scotsman* I found most heartening. Every spare moment— afternoons in stormy weather, evenings when the day was spent working outside—I gave to writing. I wrote a longer piece about remote living and sent it to the B.B.C. To my astonishment it was accepted: I could hardly believe in my luck. We celebrated with a family Burns Supper and sat round the kitchen fire, with platefuls of haggis and mashed potatoes and turnips on our knees. Jim read bits of 'Tam o' Shanter', Helen sang 'My love is like a red, red rose' and we pledged the immortal memory in glasses of rowan wine.

That small mid-winter cheer did us good, but the worry of our financial position still kept nagging away at us. It was becoming clear that the pigs were going to turn out a liability rather than an asset. We thought of selling the bungalow, with its steading and fields, and concentrating on producing eggs intensively, to carry us through till the sheep and cattle really began to show a profit. But the demand for small places had fallen away, and a decrease in our securities would mean a lessening of our overdraft at the bank. There were already signs of a tightening-up of credit facilities. Ready money was also extremely short, for the pullets which had started to lay so promisingly were slackening off.

In mid-February we sold the last of the porkers. The price they fetched was not reassuring. Two of the sows produced quite good litters of ten a-piece, but the third sow was, as we had feared, not in-pig and we had to sell her empty. We decided to put the young-sters off as weaners. By the time they were ready for the market, prices had slumped so alarmingly that we could see nothing for it but to go out of the pig business as quickly as possible. We sold the whole lot, along with their mothers, and just managed to repay the market people their advance.

It was now obvious that we should have to find an additional source of income quite soon. My writing would not be enough to bridge the gap. It was an uncertain business. I had had several short stories, on which we had pinned hopes, returned. We put an advertisement in a Glasgow paper, announcing that we would welcome a small family to share our life during the summer months. We emphasised the fact that we should like children, for this was just the place for them to run wild, and Helen was highly delighted at the prospect of having playmates in the house. But, of course, the success of this scheme was problematical. Jim decided that he would have to take on a job, once the crops were sown. Many a crofter has done this before him and there are several round about who go away to work as ghillies during the shooting season, returning in time for their late harvest. In some parts there is Forestry work available most of the year, but here, at that time, there was none. Jim would have to work in Inverness, getting home when he could, and I would carry the place on with Billy's help.

In April the man from the Board came to do the ploughing. Billy harrowed the ground with Charlie and they did very well together. We had some hectic weeks putting everything in order before Jim went off. There was the corn and grass-seed to sow, the lambs had to be dressed and inoculated, the seed potatoes prepared. Somehow or other we managed to accomplish it all. The weather was not helpful; we had one of the worst rainstorms we had ever known. One day the burn rose in a couple of hours to the size of a river, and Helen had to be kept at home till it subsided.

Then on the sixth of May we saw Jim off on the Inverness bus. It seemed very strange without him. Billy worked hard and cheerfully, but for me there was a blankness about the days. We had always shared every job, from spreading muck on the fields to wiping eggs for the van. When you work as a team the job swings along however hard or monotonous it may be. Now the rhythm had gone out of everything, and I knew Jim would be hating every moment of every day in town. Gradually, however, we adapted ourselves to our new circumstances. We each had plenty to do and the knowledge that we were fighting to save our way of life kept us going.

The sheep were causing us a lot of bother; they had got a bite of spring grass in a neighbour's grazing and were for ever breaking through to indulge their appetites, and every morning Billy had to go to fetch some of them home. Most of his days were spent mending weak portions of the fence. I took Helen to school on the carrier of my old bicycle, so as to save time on the return journey. I would leave the bicycle in the shelter of a ruined croft house near the road, to avoid having to haul it over the moor and across the burn.

Jim came home once a week. His first two days at home he spent furiously fencing with Billy. The sheep were becoming a menace. One night they raided the newly planted garden and ate a hundred cabbage and kail plants. A man who leased some grazing land adjoining ours began to complain bitterly about their depredations. Jim worried about the situation, knowing that he would have to be away some time. The banker was calling for a reduction of our overdraft, so the sheep had to be sold. We knew that this meant that the croft would never provide us with more than half a living, but the fact had to be faced.

Alec and Billy came to gather the flock and separate them into their categories—ewes with lambs at foot, and gimmers. Jim got a lift home on the evening before the sale. We shut the gimmers into a field and put the sheep with lambs into the enclosed space round the house. All night we heard them moving restlessly around. At six o'clock we were out taking a last look over them then we all went in to the market. Jim stood watching the sheep in their pens, but I couldn't bring myself to see them sold; that was a hard day.

But things had to go on. On Jim's next day at home a neighbour came, with his tractor, to open the potato drills. We planted the potatoes in the wake of the tractor and the drills were closed the same evening. Later on, this same neighbour came to prepare the turnip ground and Billy sowed the seed with Charlie.

I had to resort to all sorts of devices to get certain jobs done. There was the wringing of hens' necks, for instance. That was a thing I had never been able to do and Billy, curiously enough, would rather not attempt it either. When I had half a dozen birds to sell to the butcher, I had to put the poor creatures in a pen and ask the post to do the necessary, when his own work was done. He was always ready to help in any emergency and he took this quite as a matter of course.

Then there was the business of taking the cows to the bull. With our particular cows, who all had wills of their own, this had always meant that two people must accompany them—one to hold them on the rope, the other to open and shut gates. I therefore went, as a necessary part of the bridal party, as far as the last gate, where I waited discreetly, before resuming my duties on the return journey.

Billy spent much time, that June, cutting peats. It is hard work, skimming off the turf and cutting the blocks out of the bank. Two or three times a week I would go along in the afternoon to help him, setting the chunks in small heaps to dry. Later on we made the small heaps into bigger ones. Sometimes Sadie would come over for an hour or two and the time would pass quickly, in company. On a Saturday Helen and Bertha would join us; then the peats would fly, and the sweat would pour off Billy's face, as he struggled with all the feminine competition. There's always an element of holiday in days at the peats; it's hard work, but it's different. You're working away from your usual haunts and the air is sweet on the moor in June. On the way home we would paddle in the burn and gather handfuls of bog-cotton and huge, yellow 'butterballs' to decorate the kitchen table.

Helen came home for the holidays with a first prize for classwork and a passionate resolve to become a teacher! Each fascinating thing she learnt had to be imparted urgently to anyone within earshot. The walking to and from school had made her hardy and resilient. Some of the questions she began to ask showed that her mind was clear as a bell. A child brought up out of the reach of the multifarious distractions of town life keeps a keen, uncluttered perception. She doesn't have the adult world thrust at her in all its distorted forms, from the cinema screen, the advertisement hoarding, or the chance overheard conversation of strangers. She grows into it naturally and accepts its responsibilities as she does her food. If she wants an egg for her breakfast, she knows that the hens must be fed and cared for first. She realises that the enjoyment of a glass of milk involves fetching the cow from her grazing, seeing that she's comfortable and helping to scald the pail and basin. Even the boiling of a kettle means the gathering of good kindling sticks, and she soon learns which make the best burning. She sees life whole because she has begun by discovering its roots.

That summer we got wind of a development which was to affect the lives of almost every one of us. A meeting was called in the village hall and an official of the Hydro-Electric Board announced that the power line would be coming our way in the near future. He explained very patiently all the working of the scheme, the outlay involved, the cost of consumption and the help that could be given in the purchase of equipment. The talk at neighbourly ceilidhs over the next months was alive with comment on the plan, and practically everyone was determined to scrape the bottom of the barrel, so as to share in the benefits of electricity. For ourselves only a minimum of expense would be involved, as the house was already wired for light, and we should only need to have power plugs installed.

One amusing story went the rounds. It concerned an old countryman in the south who went to stay a night with a daughter whose house had lately been equipped with electricity. 'Well, Sandy, how did you like the electric light?' he was asked, on his return home. 'Ach', he said, 'I canna' be daein' wi' it. Kept me wakened a' nicht. It's in a bottle and ye canna' blaw it oot!'

Within a few days of the meeting, the surveyors were out on the moor and the Hydro Board's small, white van was scurrying up and down the hill road, visiting every croft. The officials were all most courteous and patient as they answered our eager questions and explained exactly where the poles were to be erected. The surveyors were scrupulously careful to avoid the arable ground. All being well, they said, we should be connected up within the year.

Ours is a bleak, forgotten sweep of upland, barely snatched from wilderness, but in the short time we have been here, we have seen it take a leap of a hundred years. A good road now links us with our market, we have a bus service and as many van deliveries of goods as we could wish for, and now—electricity. This is progress in the real sense. To equip people in their millions to mind machines and then to cater for their leisure with the provision of such hectic delights as will allow them to bear their daily boredom without complaint is not necessarily progress. To provide basic facilities for those still engaged with the earth is a thing worth doing.

CHAPTER XVI
A STORMY CHRISTMAS

Two small families made arrangements to spend their fortnight's summer holiday with us—one in the second half of July, the other in the first half of August. Each party consisted of a small girl and boy and their parents. We were confident that they would fit into the scheme of things, for they would not have chosen a small, unknown place in the Highlands for a holiday if they had been difficult to please.

Their coming involved a good deal of turn-about in the house. We made three rooms ready for their use and fitted up the living-room and the spare room off it as our camping quarters. They used the front door, and thus their part of the house was quite self-contained and they could come and go as they liked without disturbing us at our labours in the kitchen.

Ten days before their arrival, Hope obligingly calved, so that we were able to greet them with brimming jugs of cream and mounds of fresh butter. The hens were laying well and the garden was stocked with greenstuff. The foundations of good, simple meals were to hand, but I had forgotten that people living near to shops are accustomed to variety in their diet. I had to rush up and down to the gate to catch every available van in an effort to avoid monotony.

Each family had a car and they were co-operative and always willing to fetch fish and extra meat when they went off for the day. The children asked nothing better than to be left to play about with Helen in the sand-pit, climb the rowans, explore the burn, bring in Hope for the milking, help Billy cart peats home from the moor. They had all the natural child's zest for imaginative play and Billy excelled himself as host. He let them lead Charlie and ride on his back, and in the evenings they all sat in the straw in the empty byre and had shots on Billy's latest acquisition—his accordion. That was a month of hard work, but it was rewarding—our visitors became friends, with whom it was a pleasure to keep in touch.

While the house was full I had to put all thought of doing any writing aside, but as soon as we settled back into our routine I got busy again. I had had several articles about Highland and crofting life published in Scottish monthly papers, and had entered a story, of the woman's magazine type, for a competition advertised in a daily newspaper. This had been solely in the somewhat forlorn hope of making a little needed money. The prize was, I think, a hundred pounds. I hadn't really expected my story to win anything, and it didn't: it came back. But, instead of the usual rejection slip there was a polite letter expressing regret that my effort had not won a prize, admiration for the writing and confidence that, if I could 'get on to the right lines', I should be able to make a success of magazine story-writing. I was doubtful about this as I was mainly interested in writing about things I understood and loved. I was not at all sure that I understood or loved 'love' in the sense ac-cepted by the women's magazines!

I went on writing about the hills and the men and women who grow among them—the tough, obstinate, shrewd, kindly folk, who grumble one minute and chuckle the next. They haven't a shred of glamour to them, but they are real, and there are not many of them left. Already the members of the younger generation who still work in the hills are acquiring the mass-produced responses of the day; the impact of the wireless and the daily paper is slowly steamrollering them into the accepted mould. I wanted to record those whose individualities have not yet vanished, but of course it was not the way to make money.

One afternoon I was sitting at the window, writing about the reaction of an elderly crofter's widow to the coming of the electricity. I looked up, as a movement by the stile caught my eye. A tall man, wearing kilt and bonnet, was coming towards the house. In his wake was another man and behind him two women. I watched the little company approaching and saw the expressions of slight bewilderment, which no stranger manages to hide, on nearing us. Then the dogs set up a furious barking and I hurried out to greet the arrivals.

The kilted man introduced himself as the writer of the letter encouraging me to do stories for his paper. No one less like one's conception of an editor of 'pulp' could be imagined. He and all his party at once took a delighted interest in our place. They took photographs of Charlie, they inspected a new-born calf, they watched for Helen coming home across the moor.

They had come north, they explained, for a long weekend and thought they would like to look me up on their way home. We talked a little about writing matters and had a cup of tea, then I saw them off in their stream-lined car. I did write several 'love' stories after that, and an odd one or two were published, but I think this kindly editor knew as well as I did that I was not likely really to get 'on to the right lines'.

That September we had a displenish sale in our midst. It was a fine autumn day; the sunlight lay in long, pale beams across the flowering heather. It was a day for looking forward, for sniffing the earth-scent and planning next year's work. But about the croft there was only the drab confusion of buying and selling and 'flitting'. Crockery, books, pictures, all the odds and ends that had gone to make a home, stood in forlorn heaps, on top of dressers and tables. I bought a couple of peat-knives for a shilling, but I can't say I felt particularly proud of my bargain. It was as though a whole way of life were being put under the hammer and 'going ... going... gone!'

The place was bought by an active couple who turned it into a poultry farm. Practically every place in Abriachan was by that time occupied by an in-comer. In addition to the 'tomato-man', the 'strawberry-man' and the 'mink-man', there was now the 'poultry-man', and the gamekeeper's croft had been taken by a lady who kept Dexter cows and guinea-fowl and hens which laid golden-brown eggs. She was bred to country ways and it was always a delight to drop into her house for a chat and the loan of a book or a paper. Her never-failing welcome did much to help me over my spells of loneliness, when I wore the green willow for Jim.

Jim came home in time for the corn harvest at the beginning of October, and we had to rush it in between spells of storm. The potato crop was only a small one and we lifted it with the graip, taking it in turn to dig and pick. Then we went hard at the lifting of the turnips as we had to secure them before the arrival of the sheep we were to winter, for Jim had decided he would have to work away from home for another spell, in order to strengthen our financial position.

Billy would be leaving us as soon as harvesting operations were over as the Welfare people considered, quite rightly, that it was time he was embarking on a definite career. We said good-bye to him at the beginning of December and he went to work on a big dairy farm near Beauly. He had done well by us as he had always been willing to tackle anything—from taking Helen to school to painting the gable beams of the house—he had been happy with us, I think. We liked to see him laugh—and to listen to the tunes he got out of his accordion. Whenever he went to town he brought back a piece of chocolate for Jim, because he knew he liked it, and he always remembered our birthdays with a small gift shyly pushed along the kitchen table. He was growing into a big, burly fellow and he had the makings of a man of sound heart.

A few days before Christmas Jim went off to work. I took the Glen Convinth bus to town, to do the last of the Christmas shopping. The shops were warm and glittering and full of excited people, jostling one another to secure their tokens of goodwill. I felt very lonely and bewildered among the crowd so I made my purchases as quickly as possible, drank a hurried cup of tea and made for the early bus. I was thinking of our small, storm-tossed home and longing to be back in it, with Helen safe beside me. It had been blowing a gale when I left in the morning; Heaven only knew what damage might have been done in the interval. Also there would be no Jim to meet me at the gate, to take the parcels from my aching fingers, to tell me all was well, the animals were seen to, and there was a good fire in the kitchen. That was his normal welcome when I returned from a shopping expedition, but this time I would have to manage everything alone.

We picked Helen up at the schoolhouse door. As she and I emerged from the bus ten minutes later, at the crossroads, a gust of wind caught us and literally sent us spinning on our way. I don't think I've ever felt anything like the force of the gale that was blowing that night. It was from the north and it came at us like a wave of solid matter pressing on our backs. Helen was tossed ahead of me. Only my superior weight, and the weight of the bags I was carrying, kept me more firmly anchored to the road. To climb the stile, a thing normally accomplished quite automatically, became a precarious operation. It was touch and go whether we landed on the other side upright or prone in the heather.

Reaching the Macleans' house at last, we staggered into the warmth and light of their kitchen, gasping for breath. Bertha had just recovered from measles and Mrs. Maclean was not too well, but they had seen us coming from the little back window, and they had tea ready for us and a plate of pancakes. The hot drink and their kindly concern put heart into us for the last lap of the journey.

We left most of our parcels with them for collection next day and, with the loan of a stick and a torch, set off to cross the burn and make our way up the moor path. As we neared the house I sensed that something was missing. I peered about in the gloom and saw that another of our giant rowans was lying prone, its roots streaming in the wind, like pennons. We reached the back door-step and nearly stumbled over the huge, galvanised water-butt, which had been blown clean off its brick foundation. I pushed open the door and we burst thankfully into the calm of the kitchen.

There were many jobs to be done, but the first essential was warmth. I lit a candle (the windmill batteries had perished in the frosts of the previous winter and we hadn't renewed them, as the electricity was on its way), and soon had a fire going and the kettle on the spirit-stove. Then I lit the lamp and settled Helen at the fire, with a cup of cocoa and a book, while I went to see to the animals. The hens had long since gone to roost, but their crops would be well filled, for they had hoppers of mash and had only to help themselves whenever they felt peckish. I groped for the eggs by torchlight and made my way to the byre. The cows had been in all day and were ravenous and they turned their heads towards me expectantly, as I hung the storm-lantern on the hook in the roof-beam. I was thankful that hay and corn sheaves were to hand, in the false roofs Jim had made, and had only to reach up with a fork and tumble the sweet-smelling stuff down into the beasts' fodder-racks. Then I had to fetch pail after pail of water, to satisfy their great winter thirsts. Each time I staggered out to fill another pail at the byre butt I wondered if I would be blown into the next parish before I could get back with it!

I came in at last for the night and found Helen curled content-edly in her chair. She was to prove a most steadfast companion during the weeks and months we were to be alone on the croft. She never minded in the least being left by herself in the house, while I saw to the animals or went up to the gate to fetch the grocery box. Very often she accompanied me about these jobs, but many times it was too wild for her to be out. Then she would stay quite happily on her own, even after dark or during a severe thunderstorm.

Darkness, thunder, gale have never held the slightest terror for her. To grope one's way home on a pitch-black night, when the torch battery has failed, she considers fun. I've seen her stand at the window watching delightedly for the next lightning flash and count-ing the seconds till the great, satisfying crash of the thunder came. She seems to sense that these wild, natural outbursts are only rather spectacular phenomena, which have nothing to do with her inner composure.

By the following morning the gale had lessened and I let the cows out for an airing and a drink and had a look over the sheep. I had just done the feeding round that evening when the wind be-gan to rise again. It was coming in sudden squalls, straight out of the north, and it now had an edge to it—it seemed as though there was nothing between us and Iceland. The grocer's van came late that night; the force of the wind was such that it blew me round in a complete circle as I came down from the gate with the box of groceries clutched in my arms. I was a little worried, for the following day was the day of the Christmas concert at Helen's school. She was to take part in two little performances—one she had been practising for some time and one she had taken over just a few days before, when another child went down with measles. Luckily, she herself had got her measles over at the age of eighteen months! In the evening there was to be a party for all the children of the district in the Abriachan schoolroom and somehow or other I had to get Helen to both these festivities.

I lay awake that night listening to the wind tearing at the house and making the beams rock. I slipped down early in the morning and peered out into the gloom: snow was whirling out of the bitterly cold wind. I lit two candles and we had our breakfast crouched by the living-room fire. I left Helen in the warmth, while I went to feed the horse and the cows and hens. Then we had to face our two-mile walk into the teeth of the storm.

I tucked Helen's skirt into a pair of old breeches and made her wear two coats and a scarf wound round her balaclava so that only her eyes were showing. By the time we reached the Macleans we were already plastered from head to foot with driven snow. We found Mrs. Maclean far from well and I promised to telephone the doctor from the kiosk by the school. We struggled on, heads down, along the exposed stretch of road and down the long hillside to the comparative shelter of the glen where the school lay. I left Helen in the cheerfully warm, excited atmosphere of a small schoolroom on closing-day, rang up the doctor and made the return journey comparatively easily, sailing along before the wind.

It was after mid-day when I reached home again and I was so hungry that it hurt! I cooked a chop on the spirit-stove and made a big jug of coffee. Then I fed and watered all the animals liberally as this feed would have to last them until the following morning. I changed, reluctantly but dutifully, into a tidy outfit, swathed myself in coats again, and set off once, more to the school.

The little performance went off beautifully and Helen said her pieces without a hitch. Afterwards we drank tea and ate cream buns and sang carols with the children. The room was an oasis of warmth and light and colour. It seemed scarcely possible that a storm was still howling outside—but howling it was!

I knew it would be madness to attempt the long journey home and then the extra mile to Abriachan, on our own, in the blackness. So I rang up the school bus driver, who runs a car for private hire, and asked him if he would take us round. He was a little doubtful whether he'd manage to get up the hill, as it was very slippery, but said he would try. He's a great, burly fellow, always laughing and game for anything. His own bus, which he runs into town twice a week, is something of an institution. He stops at each regular passenger's gate or road-end, with a friendly toot of his horn, in the morning, and in the evening will go out of his way to put everyone down as near their door as possible, should the weather be bad. He does messages of every imaginable kind, from posting a letter to handing in a sewing-machine for repair and will load his bus with anything from bags of cement to tomato-plants and day-old chicks, in season. For everyone he has a cheery word of greeting, and should a housewife overspend herself and have nothing left for her fare he'll soothe her with kindly laughter and say, 'Ach, I'll get it again'. Small wonder, then, that such a man took us safely up and round by the loch, though his headlights and wind-screen were almost obscured by driven snow.

The Abriachan schoolroom was another oasis, a positive wonderland to come upon on such a night. A huge fire was blazing in the open hearth and a Christmas tree stood, glittering in a corner. Nearly all the children turned up, in spite of the storm, and it was a delight to watch their small, numbed faces opening like flowers in the light and warmth.

That was a memorable party; we played the Grand Old Duke of York and Blind Man's Buff and all the other well-tried games; we sang carols and Gaelic songs and we ate hot pies and iced cakes and drank scalding tea. There was a tinkling of bells outside, a huge knocking on the door and Santa Claus came in with a toy for each delighted child.

We were loath to button ourselves into our coats for the walk home, but to our astonishment we found ourselves emerging into a still, crystal world. The wind had dropped, the sky was gleaming with stars, the hills seemed enormous and remote, under their covering of shadowed white, as we walked home briskly and happily over the crisp snow. Helen sat drowsily content in the candle- and fire-light. I carried her to bed and we both slept till the bellowing of hungry cows woke us in the morning.

CHAPTER XVII
THE STILL CENTRE

JIM came home for a brief spell on New Year's Eve, but we were both too tired to stay up all evening. We went early to bed, after setting the alarm-clock for just before midnight. When it rang, we got up, poked the kitchen fire into a blaze and drank a toast in our dressing-gowns. Jim went out to fire the traditional shot from the gun, to warn the evil spirits away, and we crept back under the blankets. He had to go off again later that day. Helen took his comings and goings very calmly. She loved his company, for he could enter completely into her world. He could tell her the most fascinating stories, he could invent games out of nothing at all and he could set her the sort of problems she loved to work out in arithmetic or geography. Geography was her special passion. 'Could an elephant', Jim would ask solemnly, 'walk from Paris to the Cape of Good Hope, without getting his feet wet?' Helen would screw up her eyes, while she visualised the map, then rush to the atlas to confirm the route she had planned. The two of them were end-lessly happy together, yet after Jim had gone Helen settled quite calmly again.

For myself, I was too busy ever to feel that acute loneliness I had known sometimes, years before, when I lived among a city crowd. Sometimes, during the day, when I was alone and there was a deep winter silence everywhere, I found myself having quite earnest conversations with Hope, the cow, or with Charlie or the hens. This might have led a chance visitor to assume that I was a bit queer in the head! But I firmly believe that these creatures like the sound of the human voice, when it is not raised in anger. Hope certainly lets down her milk better after a friendly chat and the hens 'sing' delightedly when you enter their quarters uttering a stream of nonsensical remarks.

Only once, while Jim was away, did I get a bit of a scare. I was sitting by the kitchen fire knitting a sock, late one evening, when I heard heavy footsteps coming round the gable of the house. There was a scraping on the doorstep and the knob of the door was rattled. I thought—could it be Jim come home unexpectedly? He came whenever he could, even if only for a few hours, but he always gave a shout outside so that I should know who it was. My heart jumping a little, I got up and slid back the bolt on the door. I opened it and found myself peering into the long, yellow face of Charlie, the horse. Dear old Charlie! He liked to slip out of his stable whenever the door was not quite securely fastened. I stroked his nose and he stood, half in the kitchen, half out, while I filled a pail with water and scattered oatmeal in it. He drank it gratefully and I backed him out again and heard him wander off into the near field. Many times after that he came along for a late snack, and it was comforting to hear him pacing steadily round the house at night, like a policeman on the beat.

On the fifth of January came the day Helen had to start school again. We had decided that she would have to leave Glen Convinth and go to Abriachan school. Now that I was on my own, I was finding it impossible to walk with her the two miles every morning. It was usually eleven o'clock before I got back and then every job about the place had to be started almost from scratch and finished before darkness came down at half-past three.

Helen accepted this arrangement calmly enough. Her new teacher, Miss Fraser, received her with kindness and understanding and after a day or two she settled into her fresh surroundings. Miss Fraser, who was born and brought up in the district, had herself been a pupil at the school where she was now in charge. She had seen its roll diminish from over a hundred to a mere handful, but she and her sister, Miss Kate, who cooked delicious dinners for the scholars, kept smiling faces and went briskly about their work. They always made us most welcome in the schoolhouse and they understood our interest in the district. If only So-and-so were living, they would say, he would have been able to tell you so much about the place.

No local history or guide-book contains more than a passing reference to Abriachan, but the older people with the lively minds, such as our neighbour Mrs. Maclean, could make the place come to life for us. The chance visitor here, looking up towards Rhivoulich, will see only a little stone house falling into decay in its hollow on the hillside, and the bright green growth on land that had once been tended. To our eyes, thanks to Mrs. Maclean, it is the place where a cherished neighbour had her first child, when the doctor rode over on horseback, in the falling snow, from the next glen.

Likewise, the tumble of stones on the near slope to the west is the place where the good wife baked a whole boll of meal in preparation for a wedding in the family, and the festivities went on for a full week.

On the hillside, beyond our march, we can visualise the small drama that took place one day in the colourful time of the last occupant of the croft there. He was a man of many skills and one of them was the making of a dram. One day word reached him that the excisemen were on their rounds. It was winter, snow had been falling, and only that morning he'd been up the hill for a drop from the hidden 'still' to keep the cold out. The imprint of his boots had left a clear trail on the shining white ground. So he calmly borrowed a score of sheep from a neighbour and drove them up and down the hill, and round and round his dwelling, till every tell-tale footprint was obliterated. And the secret of the whereabouts of his still went with him to the grave.

Bottles and jars of the stuff were easily enough hidden in the house itself, favourite places being in the mattress of a relative put hastily to bed and said to be at the point of death, or behind the voluminous skirts of an invalid granny who couldn't be persuaded to rise from her chair.

When we watch the two burns foaming along the edges of Mrs. Maclean's east field, after a night of heavy rain, we remember how this piece of ground got its strange name 'The Island of the Cheeses'. After a downpour the field, with a burn on either side of it, does indeed become an island and, one day of exceptionally heavy spate, the cheeses that the women had made up in the shieling by Rhivoulich were carried down the burn and landed on this green patch.

On our own ground we often come on small, neat piles of broken stones and we can picture the man who worked away at them and had them ready to sell to the roadmakers, when death overtook him. This is an old land. Stone Age implements are found in the bogs and traces of very ancient habitation can be seen on the hill slopes. In spite of hydro-electricity, the telephone and the weekly bus, the links with the past are strong, and they make the present so much less shadowy and unreal.

At the foot of the hill, on the shore of Loch Ness, lies the font-like stone, its hollow always brimming with water, said to have been used by Columba for baptising the faithful. And what of the monster, that link with a very remote past? Had they ever seen it? we asked several neighbours during our early days here. Well, no, they hadn't, but they knew others who had, and seeing, we gathered, is not the only way of believing. There were so many unaccountable things in the world, anyway, that a loch monster was not such a great source of wonder after all.

The nearest we ourselves have come to seeing the monster is to have caught the reflection of its appearance in the wide, bright eyes of Sadie and Bertha. One summer evening we came on them pushing their bicycles up the hill. They had been riding along the loch shore when they came unexpectedly on a sight of the beast, cruising quietly along, quite near the bank. One or two cars stopped, they said, and a small group of people watched until the creature disappeared below the surface. It had a face like a Cheviot sheep's, Sadie said, and a sinuous, black body. Since that evening we feel we are practically one of the band of 'seers'.

Near our own march fence runs the road which the women of Glen Urquhart took to meet their men coming home from Culloden. A neighbour once found a shoe, of the type worn by the soldiers at the time of the '45, preserved in the peat, near this road. We like to think it was lost by a Redcoat in too hot pursuit of a fleet Highlander and to imagine him having to give up the chase and limp back to camp.

Among the scattered birches on the hill slope, where Helen likes to play at Jacobites and Redcoats with some of her friends, is a stone memorial to a forgotten clan chief, who died in a forgotten skirmish. On a neighbouring estate are several modest memorials, consisting of a Gaelic inscription let into a piece of natural stone. The laird responsible, a historian by inclination, wisely considered it important to record, not necessarily that a battle occurred at a certain spot but such things as the simple fact that this was the place where the shoemaker lived and worked, that even this small green field had a name.

Then there are the intangible legacies from the past. A neighbour of ours, young and active and full of fun, will still look anxiously at a heron, bird of ill-omen, flapping his way from the hill, lest he should pass too near her place. And a man is remembered who, in his youth, had to walk thirty miles in a day without speaking to anyone he might meet, to visit the only person who could cure him of the evil spell which had been cast upon him for spite.

Fear, along with its fantasies, lingers in the corners of the Highland mind, but it is a fear of the unknowable and an altogether healthier thing than fear of the calculable horrors of concentration camp, or nuclear warfare. You can live with a fear of the unknowable. It does get at the root of the thing for, at bottom, it's an honest enough acknowledgment of the existence of the mystery of evil. Once acknowledge the existence of the mystery and its manifestations, however horrible, can be seen in some sort of perspective. And it works the other way, too. Time and again, when we've been near defeat, wondering at the narrowness of the girdle which keeps happiness intact, we've been aware of a sort of hovering of friendly wings about our roof.

One snowy morning I was trudging about the steading, with armfuls of straw, when I saw a figure coming slowly down from the stile, a suitcase clutched in either hand. It was Jim! I dropped the straw and hurried to meet him. He had got several weeks' leave, before taking on a new job in spring. It had come about suddenly and he hadn't been able to warn us, even by a telephone message to the Post Office. It was better that way, the surprise was a delight in itself.

He had had to walk the two miles up the hill, from the bus, carrying his cases and was nearly exhausted. I cooked him a dish of ham and eggs and we sat talking away the rest of the morning. Then he changed into his old corduroys and dungarees and was soon tramping about the place as though he had never been away.

Jim was back just in time. The following morning we awoke to the now familiar sound of a northerly gale tearing under the roof slates. A storm of blizzard proportion battered at us all day. We struggled out three times to see to the animals. The rest of the day we spent huddled at the living-room fire, swathed in woollen garments, heating panfuls of broth and making tea and cocoa. Helen loved those days of storm, when we were marooned together cosily, in the firelight, with the world whirling madly outside the window-panes. Jim taught us to play cribbage and we went early to bed, with nearly all our clothes on and hot-water bottles stuffed down our jerseys.

We were wakened in the dead of night by the sound of water dripping on the stairs and got up to investigate. The water was pouring steadily through the ceiling at various points. Evidently the oil-lamp which we kept burning by the cistern had not provided enough heat to prevent the pipes from freezing. The overflow pipe was blocked and the water was escaping where it could.

We tried to turn on the taps in the scullery to relieve the pressure, but they were frozen, too. Next moment the water began coming through on to our beds. We lit lamps and candles, we moved the beds on to dry spots, we put every available pail and basin at strategic points to catch the drips. Every now and again a drip would stop, only to start up again somewhere else.

By this time every step on the staircase was coated with ice and going up and down in the dark was a tricky and dangerous business. We got a kettle boiling. Jim at last managed to thaw out one of the scullery taps and the drippings slowly ceased. Since that night we have always left one tap slightly on in frosty weather.

Next morning the wind had shifted to the south-west and was blowing the snow into great drifts along the road. The food van was already a couple of days overdue and we were running short of bread. I was reluctant to ask for the loan of a loaf from a neighbour, for I knew that everyone would be as short as we were ourselves. Bread is a thing one is apt to take very much for granted, total lack of it seems a calamity. That evening I baked what I hoped would turn out to be a loaf in a cake-tin. It was edible, that was all! It certainly hadn't the authentic texture or flavour of bread, but we enjoyed thick slices of it spread with butter and home-made jam.

Next day the sky was a radiant blue and the icicles along the steading roof dazzled our eyes. We went to look over the sheep and found them in surprisingly good shape. They were patiently scraping away at the snow to get a bite of heather or a mouthful of rush-tops. We filled our lungs with the cold, still air and forgot our small needs and worries. We had a sound roof to shelter us, peat and wood for warmth, milk, eggs and potatoes in plenty to keep us fed. Health and strength we knew to be the enormous benefits they really are. We were free to open our minds and let the stark beauty of hill and moor and sky strike into us.

It was like a morning before time began to tick, before life started its endless nagging. We were isolated, apart, and face-to-face with a brand-new, yet age-old, world. There was a whole, strange, unknown patterning in the crystals on a frozen blade of grass. Under the ice the water lay black and deep and remote, keeping its own counsel. This was primeval water, heedless of its function to minister to human needs. A dog barked from a croft a mile away and the silence was cracked from end to end. We made our way happily back to the job of keeping life astir, tingling with the rare refreshment that seeps from the springs of things.

As soon as the snow-plough had opened the road, John Maclean, to whom our wintering sheep belonged, came to take his flock away. They were grazing in a rushy hollow, some distance from the road. We tried to drive them slowly the half-mile to the gate, but they could scarcely move. The frozen snow had formed into heavy balls on their fleeces so there was nothing for it but to leave them where they were till they thawed out. We carried bundles of hay to them and gave them as many turnips as we could spare. Two or three days later the thaw came and they quickly recovered their normal agility.

The drains couldn't carry all the sudden rush of water and a flood rose in the byre. The water swirled alarmingly round the cows' hooves and we had to lodge some of them temporarily in the stable. Then by degrees everything settled down. The food van came and we had a meal of steak and onions and fresh bread.

By the end of the month the first larks were singing. It had seemed scarcely possible that a bird would ever sing over our fields again, yet here they were, as determined as ever to enchant us! But it was only a brief overture, for in mid-February a second blizzard struck us. It was of far greater intensity than the January one. We woke in an unusual darkness. The windows were plastered with frozen snow. We opened the door and peered out at the fantastic shapes that had risen about us during the night. Between the house and the steading there was a drift five feet deep, and the snow was already packed hard as cement.

We ate a hot breakfast, then we muffled ourselves in the heaviest clothing we could find and cut a way through to the byre. As I sat down to milk the cow the young blackbird, which had taken up its abode in the steading since the previous storm, flew down from a beam below the roof and perched on a bundle of straw near me. His bright eyes darted swift glances in my direction. As soon as the milk began to spurt into the pail he set up a tiny, inward warbling. It was one of the sweetest sounds I have ever heard. From that day on, he would greet me every morning. He was shy and shadowy yet infinitely companionable and I missed him when spring came.

Later in the morning we hacked a way to the turnip pit. The turnips were sound, under their thick cover of turf and snow, and the cows ate them greedily. The post didn't come that day. We were not surprised, for the drifts on the road were chest-high, and we knew that had there been any urgent communication for us he would have got through, though it took him till well into the night. The vanman, too, we knew would have made every effort to reach us, but it was obviously impossible. The storms always came on, or near, van-day, when supplies were at their lowest though we had laid in an emergency ration since the last blizzard wouldn't last a week.

In former times the crofts and farms always stocked up for the winter, so that they were independent of outside provisioning from October to April. A barrel or two of salt herring would supplement the home-produced oatmeal and potatoes; milk and eggs, of course, were in daily supply. Dry groceries were bought in bulk, when the lambs or stirks were sold. But today life is lived on a weekly basis and the vans go everywhere, now that there are roads that they can negotiate. Eggs are produced in greater quantities, we sell them weekly and buy our groceries weekly. When a breakdown in communications occurs, following the natural calamity of storm, we have to face a certain amount of hardship, but it is a lively experience trying to make the most one can of one's own resources.

We certainly never came anywhere near suffering real hunger. Life is sweeter near the bone. We would come in, glowing from our exertions in the snow, to eat vegetable soup and huge, floury potatoes, with a relish. Afterwards we would stretch out in our chairs by the fire, to listen to the evening news bulletin on the wireless. It was strange to hear the smooth, remote voice breaking into the stillness of the kitchen, telling of the things we had been battling with all day: we are not used to hitting the headlines. We heard of crofts isolated for days, supplies running low, telephone lines down. Well, we can do without the telephone for a while! Should there be a real emergency, sickness or accident, we know that neighbours would hack a way through any drift to get help. There are still sledges handy, there is even an old horse-drawn snow-plough on a nearby croft and there is real satisfaction in putting one's independence to the test.

What worried us, during that second blizzard, was the fact that our supply of oat-straw for the cows was running short. We had had to feed them liberally, from the turn of the year, in order to keep up their body heat, and had known that we might be faced with a shortage, for our last harvest had not been good. We had meant to buy in a load of fodder about the middle of February, but we knew that it would be some time before even a tractor could reach us. With every road in the north impassable, it might be weeks before the hard-pressed snow-plough team would come our way.

Once again Mrs. Maclean came to our rescue. She had an ample supply of fodder, she said, for her one cow. We were welcome to take as many bundles of straw as would tide us over till the road was opened. So every day we went back and forth to her barn, crossing the burn quite easily on the packed ice, each carrying two or three bundles of straw roped to our backs. It was exhausting work but it saved the cows' lives. As soon as the road was opened we got a trailer-load of straw from a farm a mile away. The tractor couldn't get into the steading, so the load had to be left at the roadside, whence we carried the whole half-ton of it down to the barn, on our backs. When spring eventually came it felt strange, indeed, to walk anywhere without an enormous burden strapped on our shoulders.

All the rest of that month we had storms, big and small. Sheep on the hill-grazing had to be dug out of drifts. We lived a hand-to-mouth life, but we kept fit and forgot what a normally planned existence was like. By the beginning of March the larks were singing again, and the black ground began to show in great, gaping patches about the fields. We looked at them curiously, for it was so many weeks since we'd seen anything but whiteness surrounding us.

An elderly neighbour died that month. The road was still closed to wheeled traffic, as it was impossible to shift the hard-packed snow by ordinary means. Jim went with the others, to help carry the coffin to the point the snow-plough had reached. In days gone by the coffins were always shouldered by neighbours, over the hill-track, to the burial ground in the next glen. The old funeral paths are still clearly visible and the cairns, where the bearers stopped for a rest, still stand. How comforting it must have been to know that one would be carried on friendly shoulders, through the sweet air, not trundled in a stuffy hearse!

By that time the grocer's van was managing to reach a point about a mile from our gate and from there we carried our goods, or pulled them on a sledge. Just before we ran out of paraffin the road was finally cleared. We swarmed eagerly into the van and laid hands on all the things we needed.

The evenings were lengthening and the moor came alive again, with peewits, snipe and curlew in possession. Slowly we discarded our heavy garments and let the soft air play about our bare heads and arms bare to the elbow. We gathered a handful of earth and let it trickle through our fingers, marvelling that it was actually warm to the touch, and dry and friable. We had witnessed one more silent miracle.

CHAPTER XVIII
THE WAY AHEAD

THAT was not to be a fully realised spring, for us. The snow was still lying on the high tops when the ploughs were set to work on neighbouring places. Horses and tractors were moving steadily up and down the small, steep fields everywhere all day and far into the darkening. But for us there was not to be a full seed-time. Reluctantly, we had had to devise a new scheme for living. We would graze sheep throughout the year and cattle during the summer months. We would buy in feeding stuff for the hens, and keep only as many as would show a profit on this basis. Our aim was to supply our essential needs—milk, eggs, potatoes, vegetables and fuel—from our own resources and to obtain cash for our further requirements from Jim's spells away at work, from the rent for the wintering and from what I could earn by writing. We had sold the van and had cut our wants down to a minimum. This shedding of the load of possessions and needs gave us a renewed sense of freedom. The van had been useful, certainly, but it had brought its own set of problems. Many a time it had refused to start, or had broken down at some crucial point on the journey home. We now found that it was the easiest thing in the world to walk to the bus when we had business abroad. There would be a layer of worry less, on the surface of our minds, and we'd have more time to watch the slow, high circling of the buzzards over the moor, and to chat with a neighbour at his field-side as we passed down the road on foot. With life being lived at its simplest level, we discovered a fresh savour in the smallest things. A fried egg, mashed turnip and a floury potato, on one's plate, was a meal to look forward to. To stretch one's fingers to a blaze of logs, during the hour before bed, was a happy occasion. Shelter, basic food and warmth, our small place would always give us. Then the mere fact of being together, the three of us, was a constant source of celebration. Further separations were inevitable, but we learnt to keep the thought of them out of sight and to live delightedly in the present. We had achieved perspective and who can fail to do that who has the sun to make him sing, the rock under his feet, the stars waiting, each night, to be wondered at?

We lost Charlie that spring. He had come through the winter in surprisingly good shape. Then one warm day, when the grass was beginning to come to a flush, he wandered into a bog and got himself caught. We tried to pull him out with ropes, but it was impossible and he had to be destroyed. It was a sore blow, but it was better for him that he should go that way rather than linger into sickness or disability. He died enjoying the freedom that he throve on and we buried him where he fell.

Summer came, a summer of real heat and brilliance. Jim was at work and I spent a lot of time writing. When Helen's holidays began, she and I practically lived out of doors. Housework came almost to a standstill. After several weeks of drought, the water system broke down, for the flow was not strong enough to work the pump. We had to fetch our drinking water in pails from the spring, and we relied on the store in the rain-water butts for other purposes. We wore the simplest clothing, which could be washed out in a minimum of water, in a pool in the burn. We ate lettuces and eggs and hardly ever lit a fire.

In the mornings we worked in the garden, and nearly every afternoon we went to the loch for a dip, as Helen loved the water and was fast learning to swim. We were both burnt gipsy-brown by the sun. We spent several days helping to pick fruit for the 'strawberry-man' and I made enormous quantities of jam. I did my writing in the cool of the evening, after Helen was in bed, and I sold several articles and sketches of Highland life to Scottish papers.

In the autumn the Hydro-Electric Scheme began to push its nose our way; jeeps and lorries careered through bog and heather, performing fantastic feats of transportation. In an incredibly short space of time a long line of poles sprang up, its straight, geometric design striking a strange note in a landscape of curves and hollows. But we quickly got used to the spectacle. The men on the job were an odd collection of types and nationalities. We boiled their dinner-kettles for them and took them into shelter on the worst days of storm. Later we stood open-mouthed to watch them swarming up the poles with climbing-irons. At last, in mid-December, we were 'lit up'. Most of the crofts in the strath were participating in the Scheme. It was cheering to see the lights flash on and off in the evening. Occasionally someone would forget to switch off a light at bed-time, and next day Sandy or Duncan would be hugely chaffed about the late hours he kept! Those who had electric fires or cookers were able to keep secret the hour at which they started the daily round, for it was no longer possible to tell, by the rising of the thin plume of smoke from the chimney-head, when the mistress had set her porridge-pot to boil!

It is, perhaps, in the winter mornings rather than the evenings that we most relish the comfort of the 'electricity'. To be able to slip from bed and flood the room with light and warmth at the flick of a couple of switches is little short of a miracle to those who have had all their lives to grope for matches in the early dark and to struggle with damp kindling sticks and paraffin oil. And to have a kettle that boils before you even have time to set out the cups and fill the teapot is certainly better than a trip to the moon. This is the sort of progress the down-to-earth Highlander really appreciates. He is still sceptical about most of the contraptions which the townsman considers essential, but something which will help him with his own fundamentals, that he is quick to prize.

That winter I began taking Helen to the village hall, on Saturday afternoons, for a lesson in the rudiments of music on the piano. We would make an expedition of it, walking over the hill on the fine days, and finishing up with a fireside chat with a neighbour before the return home. One afternoon we met the post as we reached the road. He handed me several letters, among them was one of my own familiar, self-addressed, large envelopes. 'A reject', I thought, 'I'll take a look and get it over'. I slit the seal hurriedly, meaning to forget the disappointment in the joy of the frosty, sparkling afternoon. To my astonishment, I drew out a brief, polite letter from a B.B.C. producer, which stated simply that he liked the story I had sent him, that he would use it as a Morning Story on a date in January, and that it would be read by the actor, James McKechnie.

He read the story with exactly the right emphasis and understanding, and that was the beginning of a happy collaboration. 'Why don't you write a play?' some of our friends suggested. But that I don't think I could do. I'm content for the moment that a glimpse of the Highland way of life should be borne from time to time on the back of this voice from nowhere. The truth about the Highland people is not in drama, but in the small, daily acts of living, in the long, slow rhythms which shape their lives. The spotlight is not for them. It is fitting, to my mind, that they should be 'on the air' in the morning, in the calm daylight of reality.

That Christmas I received several letters from people in far-off places—in Australia, America and the other side of Canada—who had read the little articles I had done for Scottish papers about life on the croft. I found these more heartening than the cheques the work brought me. They were mostly from Highland Scots who had emigrated and who still called themselves 'exiles'. They were proof that economic prosperity can still leave a gap in the mind and in the heart. I read lately in the paper that in the United States, among that section of the community which is satiated with the good things of life, it is quite common practice for people to take a 'happiness' pill, when they want to revive themselves, before a party. It is not surprising that thoughtful people everywhere are beginning to wonder where progress is leading us all. We can rush round half the globe, now, in a matter of weeks, provided we have a pocketful of pills to keep us in trim. Or we can sit at home and peer at the antics of the other half reflected on a tiny screen. Yet how much wiser are we at the end of the day?

There is the moon, you'll say, there is outer space. Now that we know so much about the world we live in, is it not up to us to concentrate all our energy on probing into these farther regions? But—do we really know so much about this world we've glimpsed, maybe, at second-hand? It still takes a man with a seeing eye a whole lifetime really to know the few acres he lives on.

Friends of ours, who know something of the practical difficulties we have had to overcome in the years we have spent in the hills, sometimes wonder how it is that we look so fit and are obviously so happy in what must seem to them extremely precarious circumstances. I think it is because we've learnt to set our lives to the old rhythm, we've learnt a little of the old wisdom. Men and women everywhere are burning their brains out in the gigantic effort to change the face of things, but there is, in fact, a point of submission. The small man, whose work is governed by the movement of sun and wind, of star and cloud, knows this, and so is set free. It is the marvelling eye which sees the flower pushing through the sod, beside the food-crop, and the roughened hand reaches down to gather it. Grace before meat has a meaning to folk who have nursed their potato plants to fruition and tended the cow till she yields milk abundantly. The songs that are still sung in the west all celebrate some human fundamental—birth, love, marriage, death, harvest, home-coming. Where there is no superfluity of trappings, people get the whole savour of living, and the savour so delights them that they must make a song on it.

In these hills we are still too near to 'civilising' influences. The town is only twelve miles off and we can go there every week if we will on a bus which now passes our gate. The younger people are gradually adopting contemporary habits of speech and dress. They no longer think long thoughts, or assess things in terms of human values. The members of the older generation, who were as individual as the numbered pines on the hillside, are dying out. Already some we knew in our first years here are becoming a legend. Willie Maclean has gone, and Johnny F., and now Willie Fraser and Neil, the retired schoolmaster, and John Maclean, who wintered sheep with us. Men such as these were shrewd, and could be tough and obstinate when circumstances pressed hard on them.

But they held their heads high, as members of an old race do, and their everyday speech had the far-sounding echo of poetry. Why was this? It was because they were conscious of playing a real part in the fostering of life, and the things they spoke of were real things, closely observed, as the poet, the 'seer', observes them. These people had the manners and breeding of natural aristocrats. To boast, to show curiosity or surprise, to admit to poverty, was a thing they abhorred. You could be sure of a welcome in their house at any hour of the day, however busy, and you were never allowed to go without your taste of whatever their cupboard held.

Why is it that we go so gladly to visit an old lady who has lived all her life across the burn from us? It's because we know that she'll draw us in by the hand to a seat at her fire, her eyes alight with welcome: that we shall talk of the way the larks are singing, or the corn yellowing, or of the good thing it is that the hens are back on the lay. When we talk of the weather, we shall not dismiss it as some vague nuisance in the background of our lives. We shall speak feelingly of the May frost, for it blighted the young potato crop, on which we depend so utterly. We shall congratulate ourselves on the heat in the autumn sun, which encouraged a late green bite for the cow. We know that our old lady will chuckle, as she sets the kettle simmering and patiently teaches us a Gaelic phrase ('There are some things you can't get *the feel* of, in the English!'). We know that we can sun ourselves in her warm, well-mannered geniality, that when she says 'Haste ye back!' she will mean it from the heart. She is genuinely, closely, in touch with life.

We are glad that Helen is spending her formative years under a wide sky, near to the roots and bones of things. I think, wherever she may go in later life, her yardstick will remain here. Whatever doesn't measure up to the standard of the hills she will instinctively reject. She'll need the sky's space, the cleanness of snow, the invigoration of winds blowing off the moor, the coolness of loch water and the warmth of a high-riding sun to keep her world in perspective. Already she can look and listen, and that is more than halfway to understanding. Touching will come later and then, perhaps, she will be ready to make her own contribution to things.

A child engaged in watching a chicken emerge from an egg will not bother to raise her head to watch the antics of the latest jet-aircraft in the sky. She takes aerobatics for granted. They are mostly a matter of mathematics, and can be understood. There is nuclear fission but that, too, is understandable, though the threat of its misused effects, dimly grasped from the reading of a newspaper column, is something she recoils from in dread. The real wonder is close at hand, close, yet infinitely remote, lovable, inexplicable, and thus an endless fascination.

As for living, making the most of the space between the mysteries fore and aft of her, I think the gift for that is in her hands. She loves to run out barefoot on a summer morning, to warm herself at the fire on a frosty night, to climb trees, to make things out of discarded scraps, to lie on her stomach in the grass doing nothing, but utterly absorbed in being. She's found her identity, she's in tune.

And what of our two adult selves? We've learnt this much—to work with unending patience, and to work with the rhythm of the unfathomable, never against it; to recognise the point of submission without qualm or bickering; and to make a small ceremonial about the simple acts of living. Moving this way, we can feel the light and warmth that is at the core of things fall, like a blessing, on our faces and hands.

END PIECE

IT is nearly twenty years since I set down this account of our life on the croft in the hills above Loch Ness, yet each day's doing is as bright in my mind's eye as if it happened yesterday. I am thankful that we had the immense good fortune to live for even a few years among the members of that small community which has now all but vanished. Linking hands with them, setting our lives to the rhythm of theirs, we were conscious of reaching far back into the folds of time. The signs of continuity were everywhere. The shieling huts of ninety years ago were made to the same pattern and of the very stones of those of the people of four thousand years before. Flints were picked up and used as pipe-lighters. The fields carved from the heather were not much bigger than those hacked out by the farmers who settled in the age of bronze. The sun was still the dominant factor in life. How could it be otherwise when survival depended on ripened crops and fattened beasts? The feel of veneration was still there, though the rituals of worship were long overlaid by those of Christian belief.

Now, during the last ten years or so, change has almost overwhelmed us. The green slopes of the high strath of Caiplich are nearly all deeply scarred and planted with conifers. Some of the surviving older people can hardly pass that way for sorrow. Land that was originally cleared, thousands of years ago, for food crops and has been added to slowly, over the generations, and drained and walled, this good land has reverted to timber. Some is owned and neglected by absent proprietors. A field which I look at every day from my window was taken out with the spade by a man whose grandson tells me the children had to take him by the hand to his work in the morning and lead him home at night, when his eyesight was failing. It is still green, this hard-won field, but unworked, and the heather is creeping back.

But our own old place is still an oasis. And it has been added unto. Several of its heather slopes have been drained and ploughed and brought into cultivation. Cheering, too, is the sight of the two well-worked crofts beside the little loch, with their quota of black cattle in the fields and hens strutting round the midden. Two resident proprietors of some of the highest ground are wisely allowing the old fields to be worked again and the rotational grazing of cattle and sheep is slowly building up fertility.

I suppose we are all, in varying degrees, subservient to technology now and the small green upland places are not much more than breathing and stamping grounds for those fully engaged in it. Yet there is a steadily growing demand, especially by young people, for a stretch of earth, a small, plain house, some place where a simple lifestyle can be followed. Where will they turn to when every inch is covered in holiday homes or commercial forests?

But this story of ours is no lament. It's rather a giving of thanks. And I am still, in the way life moves, very fortunate. I have only to cross the threshold to find myself walking on moss and in heather, through scattered pines and over rock, to the ridge where time stops still. Right round the horizon are the unchanging outlines of the hills. I can stoop to gather a palmful of spring water and turn to watch snow-bunting on the wing.

I am still aware of blessing. I live in the old school-house that used to seem a mansion and, from the front porch, I work what some say is the smallest Post Office in Scotland. I must use the singular pronoun for Jim, now, walks the fields of Tir nan Og. A stone of hill-top granite stands in a quiet corner of Kilianan and bears his name. His sayings are in many minds and the way into that croft of ours is still known as 'Stewart's gate'. Helen, after studying and travelling Europe-wide, never lost touch with the homeland and lives with her husband and family on a small farm only twenty miles away. She milks the Jersey for the children and is as proud of a well-doing calf and a row of sturdy cabbages as ever we were with our lambs and turnips on the croft.

I have only a garden now, but it produces all the fresh food I need, and to spare, and is a habitat for bees and chickens and a goat. What is missing is the sense of community, the sharing of glad things and setbacks by people engaged in a common way of life. So, in a sense, this story of ours is a tale of other times, almost a glimpse of legend. To us it was the reality of our lives.